1989

Infants
and Objects

Developmental Psychology Series

Series Editor
Harry Beilin
Developmental Psychology Program
City University of New York Graduate School
New York, New York

A complete list of titles in this series is available from the publisher.

Infants
and Objects
The Creativity of Cognitive Development

Hermine Sinclair
Université de Genève
Geneva, Switzerland

Mira Stambak
Centre de Recherche de l'Education Spécialisée et de l'Adaptation Scolaire and
Centre National de la Recherche Scientifique
Paris, France

Irène Lézine
Centre National de la Recherche Scientifique
Paris, France

Sylvie Rayna
Centre de Recherche de l'Education Spécialisée et de l'Adaptation Scolaire
Paris, France

Mina Verba
Centre National de la Recherche Scientifique
Paris, France

Academic Press, Inc.
Harcourt Brace Jovanovich, Publishers
San Diego   New York   Berkeley   Boston
London   Sydney   Tokyo   Toronto

English translation copyright © 1989 by Academic Press, Inc.

Translated from the French title: Les bébés et les choses
Translation by Morris Sinclair

Academic Press, Inc.
San Diego, California 92101

United Kingdom Edition published by
Academic Press Limited
24–28 Oval Road, London NW1 7DX

Library of Congress Catalog Card Number: 89-6663

ISBN   0-12-645550-3 (alk. paper)

Printed in the United States of America
89 90 91 92   9 8 7 6 5 4 3 2 1

Contents

Preface

Infants and Objects was originally published in French by the Presses Universitaires de France. The book presents observational studies based on videotaped data collected in day-care centers in Paris and in the Paris region. Over one hundred children between the ages of one and two years were observed (some longitudinally) in their familiar environment, acting spontaneously, without adult intervention, on various collections of objects. We showed that when given a choice of objects to act on, the infants organize their actions in surprisingly coherent ways that prefigure the reasoning that will later direct their logical, physico–causal, and symbolic thinking. They invent problems and themes to work on with the objects they choose, often spending the total period of observation (20 minutes) on the same idea. The studies also show that different kinds of objects elicit different kinds of activities.

The data are analyzed from a Piagetian, constructivist point of view and highlight the importance for cognitive development of the child's capacity to invent questions and problems and seek answers and solutions. In the many laboratory studies that recently have brought to light previously unsuspected abilities in very young children, subjects are generally presented with a particular problem constructed by the experimenter; our quasi-naturalistic studies emphasize a different aspect of early cognitive development.

One of the authors, Irène Lézine, is now deceased. She was among the very first psychologists in France to undertake

studies on infants, and we owe her a great debt of gratitude.
The subjects of our studies are now growing up: we hope that they are being given opportunities to develop the inventiveness, sustained curiosity, and interest they showed us during their second year of life.

H. Sinclair
M. Stambak
S. Rayna
M. Verba

Introduction

Piagetian Perspective

In this volume, we present a number of studies concerning the cognitive development of children between the ages of 10 and 24 months. Most of the research was done in day-care centers in Paris.[1] In our view, this research is to some extent a follow-up of the three studies Piaget devoted to children under 2 years of age: *The Origins of Intelligence* (1936/1952),[2] *The Construction of Reality* (1937/1955), and *Play, Dreams and Imitation in Childhood* (1946/1962).

Whatever point of view researchers and educators may adopt, all agree in pointing out that during the second year of life, remarkable changes in the behavior of children occur: Children speak their first words; they learn to walk; they attain a certain degree of independence; and their social contacts broaden. Having adopted the theoretical framework of Piaget's constructivist psychology, we find this age span is especially interesting, for it is during this time that the transition from action-based intelligence to conceptualized thought takes place.

In his earliest works, Piaget introduced an epistemological distinction between two types of knowledge—logico-mathematical knowledge and physical knowledge. This distinction corresponds to a certain classification of the sciences, but its particular meaning for Piagetian epistemology needs some explanation.

---

[1] We are most grateful to their directors and staff whose active participation made these studies possible.

[2] The second date is the publication date of the English translation.

Piaget's epistemology is realist: it accepts the existence of reality prior to any act of knowledge by a knower; at the same time, it is constructivist in the sense of postulating that intelligent beings perceive the real world that surrounds them (and, more generally, the entire environment in which a community lives) very differently, depending on the period of time and on the state of knowledge of the individual or of the society. For example, the moon was for a time considered a magic object made by a supernatural being. As a physical object, it has scarcely changed within the span of human history, but as an object of knowledge, it has now become a natural object and, more recently, a place to be visited from which rocks can be brought back to be studied in laboratories on earth.

Yet, for some societies, and for all children at a certain stage of their development, the moon is thought of as a living being who follows people when they move about and who is often kind enough to light their path when the clouds have brought on darkness. At a later stage of development, children will concur with the current views of the community in which they live (without necessarily attaining the knowledge of specialists). This construction of the real world of physical and social fact is possible only via a logicomathematical ordering of observations and through experiments that allow regularities to be noted, possibilities to be considered, hypotheses to be made and tested, and so forth. In this perspective, logico-mathematical reasoning is an instrument for getting to know the real world, the properties and behaviors of objects and of people.

For Piaget, logicomathematical knowledge is "more autonomous" than physical knowledge, which for its construction depends on a coherent logical framework. Furthermore, Piagetian epistemology is "genetic"—that is, in its theoretical constructions, it uses data from child development. The major phases of cognitive development are defined by logical criteria; this applies to the preoperative phase, the phase of concrete operations, and the phase of formal operations. How should the relations between these two kinds of knowledge be viewed? Do they develop independently from one another or in complementary fashion, one depending on the other? To seek the roots of logic in the baby's sensorimotor activities and to attribute a form of logic to the young child (even if such logic is qualified as "intuitive" or "functional") may to many psychologists appear admissible only within the framework of innate ideas that become activated as maturation proceeds. Piagetian epistemology, however, rejects the empiricist–rationalist dichotomy, as well as any discontinuity between what is innate and what is acquired. His epistemology is thus not only constructivist but also interactionist and *epigenetic* as the term is used in modern biology: All development stems as much from the capacities of the organism as from the influences of the environment. In this light, all knowledge derives from some action of the subject on his or her environment, and any experience that results in knowledge implies some activity of the subject, even if it is only in choosing what to pay attention to: He or she can confer meaning to these observations only by assimilating them into previous experiences.

Within this epistemological framework, how is the distinction between logicomathematical and physical knowledge to be made? Psychologically speaking, the distinction is based on the focus of attention of the knowing subject, either mainly on the organization of his or her actions, their order, their dovetailing one with the other, and the kinds of correspondences and comparisons they engender, or mainly on the objects on which the actions are carried out, their properties (supple/rigid, liquid/solid, hot/cold, etc.) and their behavior (rolling, bouncing, crumbling, etc.). For example, to establish a one-to-one correspondence and to know that if it is correctly done the two collections will be equal in number is a piece of knowledge derived above all from the consistent organization of actions and not from the properties of objects: the correspondence may be established between sheets of paper and envelopes, between children and chocolates, or between knives and forks—the numerical equality is deduced in the same manner. By contrast, to understand the phenomenon of flotation, it is necessary to take the properties of objects into account and to experiment: Buoyancy depends not on the way the object is placed in the water (as many children think) but on the properties of the object itself, especially its weight in relation to its volume.

In the course of their development, human beings acquire the capacity to reflect on their own actions and to be conscious of them. If this increase in consciousness is directed mainly toward the organization of the actions and their interrelationships, the resulting knowledge will be of the logico-mathematical kind; if it is directed mainly toward the way in which the objects respond to the actions of the subject and how the objects interact with one another, the resulting knowledge will be of the physical kind. Thinking about one's own actions (bodily or mental) can lead further and further away from precise content to quite formal conceptions and to the construction of pure logicomathematical systems. In contrast, physical knowledge will always be dependent on the logicomathematical framework: No experiment can lead to knowledge without the subject first having organized his or her actions and formulated anticipations or hypotheses, or without fitting his or her observations into a coherent frame of comparisons and deductions.

This is, in fact, the perspective from which Piaget described and analyzed the behavior of his own children in two works based on the same set of observations but differing in focus: *The Origins of Intelligence* (1936/1952) and *The Construction of Reality* (1937/1955). As he says in the introduction to the latter work, the focus of *The Origins of Intelligence* is on the functional development of intelligence—that is, on the formation of many action schemes and their coordination and elaboration. Parallel to this development, another aspect has to be studied: the construction of the external world—that is, the subjects' own integration of objects. In part of a third work, *Play, Dreams and Imitation in Childhood* (1946/1962), Piaget again takes up the observations made during his children's first 2 years of life and studies them with regard to the origins of representation, starting with imitative actions and noting "the parallelism with concurrent developments in intelligence." In this work, Piaget shows that development during the first 2 years of life creates the need, as well as the capacity, for the representation of ideas.

As development progresses, the need for representation increases. Even at the lowest level, a person (or any living organism for that matter) needs a certain recognition memory in order to be able to link a present experience with past experiences. When infants more or less consciously start to fix goals to be attained and to look for known means (as well as to invent new means) with which to achieve these goals, they become capable (a) of representing objects, persons, movements, localizations, and so forth, and (b) of using the representations as a means to solve practical problems. In the development of representation, the persons surrounding the baby are of prime importance. During the first months of life, infants are calmed when their mothers appear and cry when people familiar to them disappear, because they endow them with "a kind of affective and subjective permanence" (Piaget, 1937/1955, p. 13). At a later age, familiar people are "very probably the first objectified sources of causality because, through imitating someone else, the subject rapidly succeeds in attributing to his model's action an efficacy analogous to his own" (Piaget, 1937/1955, p.318).

Furthermore, so that coordinations may be made not only among the different action schemes of one subject but also between his own and those of others, a form of representative communication develops that goes beyond what the baby was capable of expressing thus far. As Piaget says, "It is by co-operation with another person that the mind arrives at verifying judgments, verification implying a presentation or an exchange and having in itself no meaning as regards individual activity. Whether conceptual thought is rational because it is social or vice versa, the interdependence of the search for truth and of socialization seems to us undeniable" (1937/1955, p. 360).

In the studies described in this volume, the social dimension discussed by Piaget has not been introduced; we observed infants on their own acting with objects. The exclusion of the social aspect from the experimental situation is not to be taken to mean that we believe that the social capacities of children develop without social interaction. In another set of studies, we observed small groups of children of the same age (Verba, Stambak, & Sinclair, 1982; Stambak, Barrière, Bonica, Maissonnet, Musatti, Rayna, & Verba, 1983), which again should not be taken to mean that we do not attribute importance to social exchanges between children and adults. No experimental situation can encompass all the live situations that go to make actions and operations possible.

The three Piaget works quoted earlier bring out quite clearly that the organization of actions (and the ensuing organization that the subject introduces into the real world) constitutes both the means of knowing the real world and, via what Piaget has called "thematization," an object of thought in itself; as an object of thought, it will become both logic and formal mathematics. From this perspective, it does not come as a surprise that stages of development are defined by Piaget according to logical criteria: In other words, they are determined by the type of organizing activity the children apply to the many problems they encounter in everyday life. The 2-year-old playing with a collection of cars and a garage may put into the garage only the little cars and set aside those that are too big. Though this behavior is not equivalent to a systematic classification made at the request of an experimenter ("put the big cars together on one side and the little cars on the other"), the child nevertheless "classifies" the cars, though maybe not exhaustively. Of course, the classification of the cars serves a practical purpose.

Toward the age of 4 years, most of the child's activities implicitly or explicitly involve this type of organizing activity— classifications, seriations, comparisons, and correspondences —and it was starting with this age that Piaget, Inhelder, and Szeminska carried out their research on elementary logical structures (classification, seriation, and number conservation) on the basis of experiments with verbal instructions. Piaget and Inhelder (1959/1964, p. 13) point out that one has to return to the system of sensorimotor schemes to find the origins of

classifications and seriations. The later structures "are foresha-
dowed very early when children pile up a number of similar
objects together or when they construct a complex object," as
well as when they build a tower of blocks. They add, however,
that "a great distance still has to be covered between these
elementary organizations and the corresponding operational
structures." In experimental situations, it is scarcely possible to
incite 2- or 3-year-olds to try to "put together those that belong
together" or to "put the sticks in order, like a staircase, starting
with the small one" or again to "put down red counters just as I
put down blue ones so that we both have the same number,
you the red, me the blue. . . ." Neither verbal instructions nor
setting the example by making a start of a classification or
seriation and asking the child to continue are very successful at
that age. And conceptual mastery of the elementary operations
of classification and seriation is rarely attained before the age of
6 or 7 years.

Piaget and Inhelder (1959/1964) described the development of the logic of concrete operations between the ages of 4
and 9–10 years, as it became clear from many experiments. In
the introduction, the links between concrete logic, intuitive
logic, and sensorimotor intelligence are briefly discussed from
a theoretical point of view. In *Epistémologie et psychologie de la
fonction* (Piaget, Grize, Szeminska, & Vinh Bang, 1968), Piaget
describes the period preceding concrete logic in terms of
"semilogic" or "unidirectional logic"; in this work also, the
theoretical framework is that of the stages of cognitive development. The question of continuity between the action coordinations of the sensorimotor period and the logic of concrete
operations is viewed mainly from the structural point of view,
though the transition to a more dynamic and psychological
approach is suggested in the 1968 work. In a sense, this
approach constitutes a return to Piaget's work of the 1930s.

The study described in Chapter 1 of the present work
was undertaken with a view to observing spontaneous activities of collecting, separating, and ordering objects, with a
number of infants all acting on the same materials and in the
same situation, though at different times.

In the field of *physical knowledge*—the organization of the real world and the knowledge of properties of objects and of regularities in the way they react depending either on the actions of the subjects or on the way they interact with other objects—the question of the link between sensorimotor development and subsequent development seems to raise fewer problems. The development of notions of physical causality seems to proceed in a more continuous though highly diversified way, and the construction of physical causality seems to continue along the lines sketched in *The Construction of Reality* (1937/1955). However, this may well be an illusion because, in general, up to the age of 11 years, causality has been less studied than logic or the logical aspects of certain pieces of physical knowledge (e.g., weight conservation). Another of our experiments (Chapter 2) thus deals with the development of physical knowledge.

A third experiment (Chapter 3) deals with an essential aspect of any *product of thought*—that is, representation by means of various signifiers. In this field also, and even more so than in logic and physics, there is a lack of developmental data. The research described here explores just one aspect of relevant behaviors—"acting as if" or pretend play.

As is well known, it is during the second year of life that children begin to act out everyday happenings outside their habitual context (e.g., pretending to go to sleep while in the middle of some activity). These play behaviors may take a variety of forms: delayed imitation, pretending, and fiction or symbolic play. In Chapter 3, an attempt is made to describe more accurately such first manifestations of the representative function. To elicit such behaviors, we presented the children with objects belonging to the familiar world of the child (actual objects in daily use or miniature objects). We supposed that these objects would lead to the kind of imitative and pretend behavior we wanted to observe. And indeed, with these materials, activities that might be classed in a category of activities leading to physical knowledge, such as those reported in Chapter 2, were rarely noted. The children did explore the objects, pushing one with the other, tapping and dropping them, but such behaviors were principally observed in very young infants, before the first "doing-as-if" behaviors. At later ages, the children grouped certain objects together, but these assemblages were generally functional (e.g., putting the spoon on the plate or mug and then scratching with it, or, at a higher level, putting together objects "for dinner" or "for washing" or for some game). Furthermore, these assemblages were not exhaustive and might change from one moment to the next, in contrast to the classifying activities noted in the study described in Chapter 1.

The study on pretend play made it quite clear that, starting from a certain level of development, the choice of materials to a large extent directs the child toward activities of a certain kind. The materials for the two other studies were chosen as a result of the experience gained in the earlier study.

The three studies presented in this volume thus fit into Piaget's psychogenetic theoretical framework. Our specific aims relate to one of the new directions taken by cognitive psychology in Geneva: focusing on the psychological rather than the epistemic subject, on discovery procedures rather than cognitive structures, on the actualization and use of knowledge rather than its epistemic characteristics. The underlying basic hypothesis is that this approach opens the way to a better understanding of the mechanism by which cognitive structures are transformed during the development of the child. This point of view attributes a preponderant role to the situations in which children are studied and entails a detailed analysis of their actions. Several recent studies fit into this theoretical framework (Forman, 1973–1975; Langer, 1980). Genevan studies directed by Inhelder et al. (1976) concern children who are older than those studied in the present research and situations in which specific tasks are requested in relation to problems with which the *researcher* is concerned, whereas our main concern was to observe actions in response to problems that the children themselves raise when dealing with some given material. Consequently, the various collections of objects used in our studies were chosen in view of the hypothesis that each collection would incite the children to ask themselves questions of a different sort. Similarly, suitable methods of investigation had to be decided upon.

Method

There is no denying the close link between theory in the broad sense and the choice of method. The study of child development is no exception to this general remark. Following a period in which the few psychologists interested in child development chose mainly naturalistic longitudinal descriptions of one or several subjects, a different approach asserted itself that reduced the changes occurring during development to quantitative changes. This approach is based on the idea that all activity is the result of outside stimulation. Even very complex activities are considered to be reducible to chains of reactions to stimuli exterior to the subject.[3] Given this conception, a laboratory-based experimental approach appeared quite adequate. This conception of development, in fact, allows the supposition that it would be possible to create in the laboratory a kind of simulation of the behaviors observed in real life. So an attempt was made to isolate behaviors and make them happen in the laboratory by submitting the observer and the subject to highly structured and restrictive procedures. Such investigative methods go with a variety of evaluative procedures and ways of measuring the responses of the subject and yield a quantification of the observed behaviors.

This way of quantifying the changes observed during the development of the child was frequently criticized by authors who, following Wallon and Piaget, adopted constructivist theories by putting the accent on successive organizational levels of behavior and on qualitative changes. Researchers who follow this trend generally adopt observation methods that are closer to naturalistic studies than the laboratory studies.

New impetus was given to naturalistic observation by progress in ethology. Initially, the behavior of animals was observed in their natural habitat (Lorenz, 1941; Tinbergen, 1963). This approach was subsequently applied to the study of child behavior (see Smith, 1974) and more particularly to the

---

[3] For a discussion of this model, see Overton and Reese (1973).

study of social interactions (Lamb, 1977). These studies un-
doubtedly uncovered a mass of new facts and led to many new
explanatory hypotheses. Nevertheless, the observer of animal
behavior in nature as well as the observer of child behavior in
the course of development came (and still come) up against
great difficulties in the matter of the treatment of the collected
data. There was considerable temptation to apply to field
observations the same quantitative treatments that had been
used in laboratory research. Only gradually were adjustments
made in procedures on the one hand and in the treatment of
the collected data on the other. Observations of children were
thus increasingly being made in situations arranged by the
researchers. These situations were designed to be as close as
possible to the usual life of the child, but in accord with their
working hypothesis, the researchers limited their field of
observation in time and space. In the collected data, attempts
were then also made to go beyond the quantification of isolated
behaviors by seeking to define a more comprehensive organization of behaviors. More recently still, under the influence of
socialization studies on children, sequential analyses were
made, with a view to bringing to light discovery procedures
rather than structures. In such analyses, the time elements of
duration as well as succession clearly need to be taken into
account. This consideration has been facilitated by the advent
of film and videotape observation techniques that make microanalyses possible.

The principal aim of the three studies was to understand the discovery processes in relation to the world of
objects. In order to abide by this aim, observations were made
in situations that did not hamper the children's activities; they
themselves took the initiative and made plain what problems
they were concerned with. In creating these situations, we let
the children act spontaneously, but we chose with care the
materials available to them, keeping in mind the particular aim
pursued.

Our observations were made in day-care centers where
we went regularly. The children knew us well; they were
accustomed to our being there. We observed them in the rooms

they habitually stayed in. During the observation sessions, our intention was to adopt an attitude that was not unlike that of participants: We closely observed the course of activities without intervening directly. Throughout the session, we showed interest in the children's achievements and responded by gestures, smiles, and attitudes that came to us spontaneously whenever the children addressed us.

Except for the study on symbolic play, which was the first to be undertaken, all our research was done with the help of closed circuit television. Our observation sessions lasted about 20 minutes.

After the very first screenings of our films, it was clear that in the situations we arranged, the children were active and interested by the material proposed; their attention hardly wandered during the 20-minute observation periods. However, methods for analyzing the transcriptions of the tapes were arrived at only very slowly. Throughout the process, we were guided by theoretical considerations. Because our focus was on discovery procedures, on *how* the new acquistions come about, simply counting the occurrences of this or that isolated behavior was not sufficient. We sought to identify sequences in which successive actions might indicate a coherent organization that could throw light on our working hypothesis. Within each of these sequences, each action appears limited to the preceding one; an analysis of the successive links often gives a clear idea of the solutions the children bring to the problems they have raised.

The microanalyses showed that the same type of sequential organization is observed with different children and also with the same child at different times of the same observation session, so that an interpretive value may be accorded to such sequences. They also showed that the organization of the sequences changed with the ages of the children studied (between 18 and 24 months). The analysis of the changes clarified the development of the cognitive aspects we were interested in (logical, physical, and symbolic).

This type of analysis thus provides insight into (a) the adaptive solutions the children are capable of reaching for the problems they raise for themselves during several phases of their development and (b) the genesis of various cognitive functions.

In this volume, we present three foci of research. In Chapter 1, "Infants and Logic," we observe the early organization of activities, such as putting together, separating, substituting, and making one-to-one correspondences. In Chapter 2, "Infants and Physics," we observe infant experimentation and the construction of new objects. And in Chapter 3, "Infants and Symbolization," we learn about the child's knowledge of events and familiar objects and about the child's capacity for detaching this knowledge from its reality context.

CHAPTER 1

Infants and Logic

M. Stambak, H. Sinclair, and M. Verba
in collaboration with
L. Moreno* and S. Rayna

* Psychologist, Mexico City

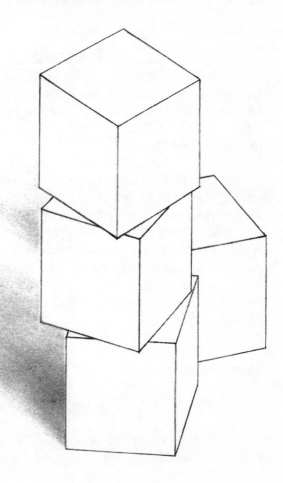

Starting from Piaget's work and from our own observations in day-care centers, we undertook to study the following problem: Can a progressive organization of behaviors, such as ordering or seriating objects, establishing correspondences among objects based on similarity, or establishing one-to-one correspondences as a preparation for the concept of number, be shown to exist at an early age?

Method

One study was carried out by a group of researchers of the Centre de Recherche de l'Education Spécialisée et de l'Adaptation Scolaire (CRESAS), and additional work was carried out in Tehran (Verba, 1981).

The materials presented to the children were chosen rather intuitively. The choice was clearly important in influencing the kind of behaviors one might hope to observe. To incite "prelogical" behaviors, it appeared that ordinary objects that the children knew well should not be used because they would probably give rise to imitative and make-believe behaviors (see Chapter 3). Furthermore, in order to incite behaviors such as collecting, ordering, and creating correspondences, it was essential to present several collections of nearly identical objects.

Materials

a. In Paris, the following materials were used:

- A series of six nesting cubes with edges measuring 2–6 cm

- A series of six cylindrical rods of natural-colored wood measuring 5–20 cm in length
- A series of six balls of modeling clay measuring 1–5 cm in diameter.

b. In Tehran, the materials were slightly different:

- A series of five nesting cups or bowls measuring 5–10 cm in diameter
- A series of five balls of cork proportional to the cups but smaller in diameter
- Three cylindrical rods 20 cm in length.

In the examples taken from the protocols, cubes and cups are indicated by **C**, rods by **R**, and balls by **B**. The smallest object of a series is designated as number **1**, and the largest as **5** or **6**. Thus, **B1** means the smallest ball, and **C5** the fifth cube or cup, starting from the smallest.

Population

a. In Paris, all observations were made in two public day-care centers with children aged 10 to 24 months. We recorded 47 observation sessions distributed as follows:
1. In longitudinal observation, three children totaled 25 sessions.
K. was observed at ages 10;4—10;20—11;16—12;5—14;23—16;4—17;22—18;13—22;0—23;17—24.
F. was observed at 9;28—10;14—11;10—14;17—15;28—18;14—20;21—23;10.
V. was observed at 13;15—13;21—14;15—15;23—17;5—24;2.
2. Other children were seen only once[1]:

---
[1] At the same ages, no differences in behavior types were found between children who used the materials only once and those who used them several times.

Age in months:	9/10	11	12	13	14	15	16	17	18	19	20	21	22	23	24	Total
Number of children:	1	1	2	1	—	1	3	—	1	4	—	2	1	1	4	22

The total number of observation sessions was distributed as follows, according to the ages of the children observed:

Ages in months:	9/10	11	12	13	14	15	16	17	18	19	20	21	22	23	24	Total
Total number of observation sessions:	5	3	3	3	3	3	4	2	3	4	1	2	2	3	6	47

b. In Tehran, three groups of children were observed. The children were aged 12, 18, and 24 months, and there were 5 to 7 children in each age group.

Procedure

It was important to make our observations without interfering with the children's own activities, and to observe in such a way as enable us to discern the problems that the children would raise for themselves. For this purpose, we put the children on the floor with the objects strewn at random. Two researchers made the observations. One of them was seated next to the child and closely followed the child's actions but never intervened unless requested to do so by the child. The other researcher worked the video camera.

Analysis of the Observation Protocols

It is well known that the transcription of videotapes raises numerous problems. We do not claim to have made an exhaustive analysis but endeavored to make as faithful as possible a transcription of object manipulations, leaving aside body attitudes and facial expressions.

All the children's actions were noted seriatim and entered in various columns in each case, in order to show which object was being handled in relation to which other object.

A short extract of notes on K. at 16;4 illustrates her use of balls and cubes.

1st Object	Right hand	Left hand	2nd Object
B6	puts into		C5
B5		puts into	C6
B6	takes out of		C5
B6	puts into		C4
	raises		C4–B6
C4–B6	puts into		C6–B5

The cumulative data appeared to indicate three periods in the development of prelogical activities. Between the ages of 9 and 12 months, the first spatiotemporal relationships are worked out, and actions become differentiated according to the type of object that is acted upon. From 12 months on, prelogical activities appear. Around the ages of 16 to 18 months, many changes occur, leading to a further period of prelogical activity between 18 and 24 months.

We were able to observe a spectacular development of activities of the prelogical type beyond all expectation. In this chapter a description is given of how in the first period (between 9 and 12 months) the first spatiotemporal relationships are worked out together, with the first actions differentiated according to the class of object. The account of these first coordinated actions are followed by a detailed description of the observed prelogical activities. The latter fall into two parts: (1) before and (2) after the age of 16 to 18 months, this age apparently being a period in which far-reaching changes in prelogical organization occur.

First Differentiations:
Between 9 and 12 Months

As has been generally observed, the most frequent actions with objects at this age are touching, scratching, throwing, tapping, lifting, turning, and so forth, and our records concur. In this period (9–12 months), the observed actions are mainly still indiscriminate in the sense that any of the objects present may give rise to the aforementioned actions.

K. at 10;20 explores the three kinds of objects, as follows.

> *Rods:* K. takes R3, beats on the floor with it, throws it away. K. picks up R3 again, shakes it, taps with it on C1, throws it.

> *Balls:* With B4, K. touches B6, which is on the ground. With the other hand, K. takes up B6, presses B4 on B6, throws down B6, picks it up again, puts it into her[2] mouth, bites it, lets it go, puts her hand on B6, takes B2 in one hand, presses it on B6. With the other hand, K. takes B4 and presses both on B6.

> *Big cube:* K. takes, lifts, shakes, and lets go of C6. K. takes it up again, looks at it, puts it down, taps the inside of the cube with her hand, then scratches the outside, overbalances the cube on its side.

> *Little cube:* K. puts her index finger inside C1, looks at the cube, lets it go, takes it up again, looks at it, puts it into her mouth, takes it in both hands, puts both index fingers inside.

Like the other infants of this age, K. makes a certain choice of activities applied to the three kinds of objects in

---

[2] Her, his, she, he, etc. are used throughout according to sex when the reference is to a known individual child. Occasionally, "he or she" pronominalizes the infant in general passages. For clarity and economy, dolls and teddy bears are pronominalized as "it." (Translator's note)

function of the objects' properties: She mainly taps with the rods. When she handles the balls of clay, she presses on them with her hand, or else she presses one ball with the other. The cubes give rise to an exploration of the inner space (with the whole hand for the large cube and with the index finger for the small one) and of the outer surfaces.

At the same time, cyclical actions were observed that are repeated either with the same or different objects (often belonging to the same class). This is already apparent in the examples given, but here are some further examples that also are typical of this age group:

F. at 9;28 takes C3, touches C2 with it, beats C4 with it, looks at it, lets it go, takes it up again, beats the floor with it, beats B6 with it, lets it go.

K. at 10;4 touches C6, then C4, then C3, then C5. K. looks at the researcher, then at the toys (on the floor), then at the camera, then at two balls of clay (to the right), then at B4 (left), then again at the two Bs. K. scrapes B6 with her index finger, looks at B6, scratches C4 with index and thumb.

F. at 10;14 takes B2 and throws it away, ditto B1 and B3. F. takes, shakes, and lets go of R6, then C6, and then R4.

These kinds of actions, however trivial they may appear, become important in the light of developments observed later. All the infants showed a tendency to carry out an activity comprising several linked components (e.g., taking, tapping, throwing) on the same object (or sometimes on two objects) and the tendency to repeat the same simple action on a whole series of objects one after the other. After a period during which the objects seem an integral part of the action, there are indications, as is seen in the examples quoted, of a dissociation between objects and actions: It seems that when the actions become more complicated, there is room for equivalences between actions and equivalences between objects to develop.

This type of activity (which, depending on the child, may last for one or two sessions) is soon followed by more elaborate spatiotemporal combinations. Thus, at about 11–12 months, actions such as *putting on top of* (e.g., one cup on another) or *putting in touch horizontally* (e.g., putting two rods end to end) are frequently observed. Among all the combinations observed at this age, the one that for a long period remains dominant is *putting one object into another*. What makes this action so important for the child? One may speculate as follows: Putting one thing into another is an activity with many constructive meanings. It creates a new complex object (a topological entity that can be displaced as one thing, without falling apart). It is a sure way of localizing an object—in fact the only way, as long as spatial coordinates have not yet been constructed. And it is a very direct way of comprehending relations such as bigger–smaller and content–container.

Here are some typical examples:

F. *at 10;14* takes C2, puts it into his mouth, puts it into C6, takes it out of C6, puts it back into his mouth, and then back into C6. F. takes B2 and puts it into mouth, looks at it and puts it back in mouth, tries to insert it into C3 (the ball is too big), and all topples over.

K. *at 11;16* puts B2 in mouth, tries to insert it into C4 (lateral opening), sets C4 upright, and puts B2 into C4, puts C2 in mouth and then into C4.

F. *at 11;10* puts R4 in mouth and then into C6. F. tries to put R6 into C6, puts it in mouth. F. tries again to put it into C6, puts it into mouth, then abandons it.

Note that all three classes of objects (balls, cubes, and rods) are used as contents and that all the cubes are used as containers.

The action of putting in mouth remains frequent among the older subjects when they have difficulty in putting one object into another, but then it seems to fulfill a different function. After an unsuccessful effort at putting one object into another, they put it in their mouth as if by this action they wanted to make sure that the object is a possible content.

When *putting into* is done with cubes, we have an attempt at nesting. Attempts to put a larger cube into a smaller one were rarely observed; usually it was one of the smaller cubes (C1, C2, or C3) that the infant tried, not always with success, to put into either C5 or C6. In addition, and this is more important, the subjects were observed to explore the dual character of one of the cubes (i.e., its peculiarity of being both or either container and/or content).

The interest in the dual relationship, which older children construct when they explain verbally that B is at once larger than A and smaller than C, was observable in K.'s actions, who, at the age of 10;20, successively put C1 (the smallest cube) in her mouth and then her index finger into C1. At the next session (11;16), she alternated between putting C1 into a larger cube and putting a small rod into C1, as if she were intrigued by the double role of C1 as container and content.

K. *at 10;20* puts stretched index finger into C1, lifts it, looks at the cube and lets it go; takes it up again, looks at it, puts it into her mouth. During the same session, she takes C1, puts into mouth, explores it with her lips, puts index finger straight into it and throws it away. At the end of the session, she takes C1 and puts it into her mouth, explores it with lips, puts index finger into it, puts it back into mouth, then tries to place it onto C3, but it falls off. She takes C3 and tries to cover C1 with it.

K. *at 11;16* takes R1, introduces it successively into C1, C3, and then again into C1. K. then lets go of R1 and puts her index into C1. She plays for a while with R2 and then puts C1 into C3. For a considerable time, she tries to extract C1 from C3 without success. Then C1 comes out all by itself during a manipulation of C3. K. puts C1 back into C3, then takes B1 and puts it into C3–C1. Several times more during the same session, she puts C1 into C3 and R1 into C3.

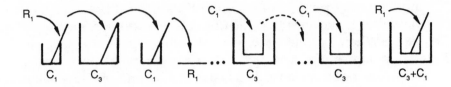

From the earliest successes with *putting into*, the child tries to take the content–object out again (by taking it out with the hand, and not yet by tilting the container). Both the in and out action may be accompanied by verificiation through putting in the mouth, but in a more fugitive way than during the unsuccessful attempts at putting one object into another. Examples of *putting in* and *taking out* were very frequently encountered. Here are two:

F. *at 10;14* puts R3 into C6, takes it out, puts it in again. F. taps with C6 on the floor while R3 is still inside, lets C6 go, and takes R3 out.

K. *at 11;16* takes C1 and puts it into C4 (which already contains B2), takes it out again, brings it to her mouth, looks at it, puts her index finger into it, puts it back into C4, puts her hand into C4, takes out C1, puts it back again, tries to take it out once more, does not succeed, and abandons it.

It is tempting, though not necessarily correct, to distinguish two aspects of these behaviors: on the one hand, a concern with the properties of the object, which alternately may be container or content, and, on the other, a concern with actions of which one cancels the result of the other (putting in and taking out).

During the earliest sessions at which we observed examples of *putting into*, the actions do not yet form sequences, although they may be repeated several times during the same session. Generally, the child is satisfied with putting one object into another and taking it out again immediately after; the activity of *putting into* does not yet seem to have any special importance and makes its appearance among other activities (beating with one of the rods, shaking an object, throwing it, moving in the direction in which one of the balls has rolled, etc.). But very soon, *putting into* will acquire an iterative character with one object being put in a container, followed by another one, and so on. During the same period, another activity acquires iterative character (i.e., that of using one of the rods to touch, one by one, different objects belonging to the same class). We noted that with our experimental material, these iterative actions became more and more frequent (in comparison with other types of actions) and increasingly structured. On the theoretical level, one may point to the epistemological importance of iteration (a) in the construction of relationships of order and class and (b) in the construction of series of natural numbers (one, one plus one, two plus one, etc., by way of cardinal iteration; and one, the first; another one, the second, etc., by way of ordinal iteration). The convergence of the increasing frequency and clear evolution of these iterative actions among our subjects between 12 and 14 months and their epistemological prominence (Gréco, Inhelder, Matalon, & Piaget, 1963) seems of considerable interest.

The Prelogical Organization of Activities

At the age of about 12 months, as indicated, these iterative actions of prelogical type make their appearance, and their development was followed in our observations until the age of 24 months. These behaviors are progressively organized and, between 18 and 24 months, lead to collecting, nesting (cubes or cups), and establishing one-to-one correspondences. In this development, we distinguish two periods: before and after the age of 16–18 months.

From 12 Months to 16–18 Months: The Earliest Iteration of Actions

During this period, iterations of actions are of two kinds: One tends toward collection: putting together or uniting dissimilar objects in a container, usually by taking them one by one. The other prefigures distribution: localizing and individualizing objects belonging to the same collection by touching them one after the other.

Putting Together, Uniting, and Separating

Because of their later evolution, we consider the behaviors now to be discussed as prefiguring *putting together* and *collecting* in the full sense of these terms.

From about 12 months on, *filling* is frequently observed: Three or four objects of different kinds are placed in one of the largest cubes. This iteration of the action of *putting into* seems to be carried out in order to observe the result, which is an increase in the number of objects put together inside the cube and/or a decrease in the amount of empty space inside the cube. The children do not yet choose the objects they put into the cubes. They take what comes to hand, interrupting themselves occasionally in order to put an object into their mouth or to take out of the cube an object they have just put in, or again in order to look at the inside of the cube.

Here are some examples of this kind of behavior:

F. *at 11;10* takes C3 and puts it into C5, takes out C3 and
    puts it back in again. F. takes R6 and taps with it
    inside C5, puts it into his mouth and then lets it go,
    takes R1 and puts it into C5–C3.

M. *at 12 months* takes C4 and successively puts B3, B2, and
    B1 into it. At this point, the largest ball exceeds the
    capacity of the cup. He tries to shove it down into the
    cup but fails. He takes it out and puts it down. Then
    he also takes out B2 and B1. Starts again with smaller
    objects (puts into C4 successively B1, C1, and B3).

Takes a rod and pushes down B1, which was protruding slightly, then the collection overbalances and the cup empties itself.

While filling a cube or a cup, the child may take out one object in order to replace it with another.

K. at 12;5 takes R1 in one hand and R4 in the other, puts them into C6; takes B3 and puts it also into C6; takes R4 out of C6 and abandons it; takes R3 and puts it into C6–R1–B3.

V. at 13;14 takes B2 and puts it into C4, which she shakes and then puts down. Then she also puts in B3; takes B2 out of C4–B3, puts it into her mouth, puts it back into C4–B3, takes it out again, and abandons it. She takes B2 and puts it into C4–B3, then takes R6 and puts it into C4–B3–C2.

Just as *putting into* is accompanied by the inverse action of *taking out*, so *filling* is twinned with *emptying*, the latter being done by taking the objects out by hand, one by one, and not by turning over the cube or cup.

K. at 12;5 first puts B1 and R5 into C6, then adds B3, B2, and C1. She takes out first R5 and then C1, takes R3 and puts it in C6, then completely empties C6 by taking out, one by one, B1, R3, B3, and B2. She puts her hand back once again into C6, but nothing is left.

During these activities, it happens that a child is interested in putting small cups into larger ones, a behavior that was observed already during the 10–12-month period. The child is thus led to carry out her or his first nestings. During this period from 12 to 16 months, we encountered this interest more frequently at Tehran, for the bowl-shaped cups are easier to put one into the other with the opening either upward or downward than the cubes.

T. at 12 months puts C1 into C3, takes it out and puts it into C2, takes it out again, and again puts it back into C3. A little later, T. puts C2 into C5, takes it out and puts it into C4, takes it out and puts it back into C5. Then she puts C4 into C5 and adds C2, thus achieving the triplet C5–C4–C2.

D. at 12 months puts C2 into C3, takes it out. D. turns it over and puts it back upside-down into C3, takes out C2 again and puts it down, takes C3 and puts into C3–C4, thus achieving the triplet C4–C3–C2.

V. at 15;23 puts C4 into C5, touches C2 with his index finger and puts it into C5–C4. V. looks at C6, takes it, and beats with it on C5–C4–C2.

To Individualize and Localize Objects

Together with the earliest fillings, behaviors appear that will evolve toward distribution. They are perhaps prefigured by the action of touching successively several objects by hand, but we do not wish to insist on this point because we have no way of deciding whether the action of touching is intentional, for it happens quickly and easily in the general flow of movement. By contrast, the activities that now appear are clearly intentional because they are accomplished by means of an instrument, nearly always one of the rods. The child presses with a rod on several objects one after the other, or else the child presses down with it inside several cubes or cups, one after the other, without letting it go. This action of using a stick to touch several objects one after the other does not bring about any changes among the objects, unlike the act of filling. For the children, it seems to have the meaning of individualizing the objects and noting their position in space; at the same time, it assigns to each object a position in a temporal order (the first there, the second there, the third there . . .).

P. at 12 months touches B3 and then B2 with a rod. After various manipulations, he holds one of the rods in one hand and with the other brings closer B2, B3, and B4, and puts them in contact with the rod.

K. at 12;5 takes R4, looks at it, and keeps holding it in her left hand. With the other hand, she takes C4. With R4, she firmly touches C4, held up in midair. Then, using the rod, she firmly touches C5 and C3 (on the floor), and again C4 (in midair) and lets go C4. . . . She presses down on the inside of C4 (now on the floor), then of C2, then of C6.

As is apparent from the examples, the iteration of *touching one by one* is usually done with objects of the same class, whereas the action of collecting objects one by one in the same container is done with objects of various classes. The action of touching one by one thus individualizes the serial construction "one, another one, another one . . ." while implying a choice of identical objects (if the difference in size is ignored).

Combinations Involving Putting Together and Individualizing

During this same period, action sequences can be observed that combine the two kinds of activities (filling and individualization) and that seemingly prefigure the creation of correspondences observed from the age of 16–18 months on. These behaviors also clearly show intention. Here are some examples.

During filling actions, the child may take not only objects lying on the floor, but also objects that have been placed in another container. In this way, one container is replaced by another.

V. at 13;21 takes B6 out of C6 and puts it into C5, takes up and holds R6 in her hand, and with it firmly touches the inside of C5–B6 and of C6.

In other instances, one container-object is replaced by another:

F. at 14;17 puts R3 in C5, taps with it inside the cube, takes it out and holds it in his left hand. F. takes R1, makes a gesture toward his mouth, then toward C5; F. beats his knee with it, then puts it into C5, lifts up C5–B1, and shakes it.

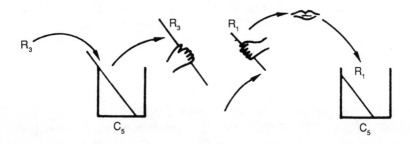

M. at 12 months introduces B2 into C4, takes it out and grasps B4 with her other hand. M. taps B2 against B4 in midair and then puts B4 into C4.

V. at 15;23 takes R2 and puts it into C5, then takes R1 and puts it into C5–R2 without letting it go. V. puts it end-to-end with R2 (which is in C4), lets go of it inside and immediately takes R2 out of C4, in which R1 remains.

By bringing together two similar objects before replacing one with the other as content, the children very clearly show their preoccupation (a) with individualizing the members of a class of objects, (b) with comparing them, and with dealing with them as interchangeable.

The following example illustrates another variant of the interchangeability of the contained object:

B. *at 12 months* takes C3 and uses it to cover first of all B4
and then C1 (which is almost invariably used as
content), then lifts up C3 and takes C1, which he puts
into C5, then takes hold of C3 (turned upside down)
and places it onto C3 in C5.

The container cup, which most frequently is the *passive*
object (which receives various contents), in this instance becomes the *active* object (which is actively used), to cover various
content objects. During the activity of *touching one by one* with a
rod, the children sometimes let go of the rod within a container
and take other rods, in order to put them together in the same
container. In this way, they simultaneously treat several containers as separate elements of the same class and bring
together several rods inside the same container.

V. *at 12;8* puts R3 into C6, takes it out again and, with her
other hand, lifts up C5. V. presses down with R3
inside C5, then inside C6 (on the floor), then once
more inside C5. She lets it go inside and puts down
C5–R3, then adds R2 and R6 to C5.

The various procedures noted lead to the first efforts at
achieving *coupled pairs* (either two rod–cube pairs, or two
ball–cube pairs).
Here is an early example:

E. *at 13;19* puts B3 into C5, lifts them up and takes out B3. E.
puts it back in again and takes it out again; puts
down C5 and puts B3 into C4, then takes B6, looks at
it, and tries to insert it into C3, but C3 turns over and
empties itself.

This example clearly shows an attempt to create a
couple of ball–cube pairs, but when the cup overturned, E. did
not persist.
The following examples are taken from K.'s efforts at
16;4. Throughout the whole observation session, she seems to
have been mainly concerned with setting up a series of pairs.

E. at 16;4 takes B5 in one hand and B6 in the other right at the beginning of the session. She tries to introduce B5 and B6 simultaneously into C5, which already contains B1 and B2 (the beginning of a collection). Not succeeding, she simultaneously distributes one in C5 and the other in C6 (to make a second ball–cube set). She then takes B6 out of C5 (which still contains the two small balls, B1 and B2) and puts it into the empty C4 (third ball–cube set). She then takes one of the small balls (B2) out of C5 and puts it into the empty C3 (making four pairs). K. also takes B1 out of C5 (which now becomes empty) and puts it into C6–B5 (thus canceling two constituted pairs).

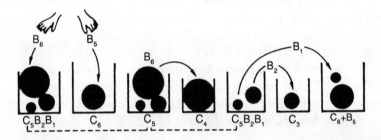

A little later during the same session:

She takes R5 in one hand and R2 in the other, and puts both of them simultaneously into C5 (start of a collection?). She then takes R6 and puts it into C6 (first rod–cube pair), then takes R3 and puts it into C1 (second pair). Then, one after the other, she takes R5 out of C5, then also removes R3 from C1, and puts it into C4. K. continues for a while to make various R–C pairs.

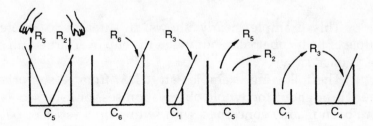

K. thus persisted in her efforts to set up a series of pairs, starting with rod–cube pairs. During this session, K. does not yet try to establish one-to-one correspondences between members of two classes. In fact, at times, she takes a pair apart to start some other activity (e.g., collecting). What is striking and indeed astonishing, however, is the tenacity with which she goes about setting up her series of pairs.

It seems clear that during the period described, the children's attention is centered on the organization of their actions. The actions in themselves are simple and consist mainly in taking the objects one by one, choosing objects that can be contents, putting them in containers, and taking them out again. The properties of the objects concerned are few and equally simple: their resemblances and differences, their equalities in relation to a certain action, and their quality as containers or potential contents. Qualities such as being either fragmentable (balls of clay) or capable of being used as a tool (rods) do not appear to interest the children very much in this situation. Their attention bears rather on the repetition and variation of action sequences, and on results obtained. The impression is strong that the child is thinking ("I put one, and another one, and another one, and the pile gets bigger"; "there is one, and another equivalent one, and another equivalent one"; "that's the first, and the next one, and the next one"; similarly, "one and one make a pair, and another one and one make a similar pair"; etc.). As we show in the next section, during the following period, this centering on the logical or prelogical organization of actions, with its immediate consequences for the organization of objects, continues to develop and reaches a convincing prefiguration of the operations of classification and seriation and the creation of one-to-one correspondences.

From 16 to 24 Months: Collecting, Nesting, Establishing Correspondences

From about 16 months on, there is a change in the action sequences, and behaviors such as collecting, nesting, and establishing correspondences are seen.

Collecting

Filling a large cube with objects belonging to various classes soon gives way to collecting objects belonging to the same class (differing only in size). During the *filling* period, the child created a new entity out of dissimilar objects, and treated it as a new topological whole (a filled cube). From 15–16 months on, the physical container (e.g., the large cube) is no longer needed. The child may also take the objects and put them either into the hand of the researcher or on the floor in a special place (e.g., between the child's legs). Putting the objects into the big cube no longer has its special status as a material collecting point; it can be dispensed with, or another place may also serve (the objects are of course still placed close together). At the same time, the children no longer collect different classes of objects in order to put them together; collecting is now restricted to objects of the same class.

Filling thus disappears in favor of an activity that can be called *collecting*, which consists in putting similar objects together. Initially, several objects are collected, but the child does not try to make an exhaustive collection of a particular class.

F. *at 15;28* puts four rods (R2, R3, R5, R6) one after the other into his left hand. Then F. takes up other activities.

L. *at 16;22* puts five balls (B1, B6, B2, B5, B4) one after the other into the researcher's hand. Then L. takes them out one by one and places them on the floor between his legs.

V. *at 15;23* puts four balls one after the other behind her.

V. *at 17;5* takes C6, and with rapid movements puts in B2, B3, B5, and B4.

J. *at 19;4* gives the researcher four rods, one after the other.

Starting with this period (18–20 months), the first *complete collections* are observed: The child puts all the rods into his own or into the researcher's hand.

K. at 18;13 puts all the rods one after the other into the
researcher's hand. During the same session, she puts
four balls into C6.

V. at 19;3 puts all the rods into his left hand, and later puts
four balls into C5.

At a slightly later period (between 20 and 24 months),
several children were observed to make complete collections of
all three classes of objects (rods, balls, and cubes).

What is striking in these activities is that they are carried
out swiftly without any hesitation. The impression is that the
intention to bring all the members of one class together was
clearly formed beforehand.

I. at 21 months puts all the balls into C5.

F. at 20;11 puts all the balls into C5.

F. at 23;11 puts all the rods into C6.

This "classification" is still of course far from satisfying
the criteria of a logical classification (with notions of class
inclusion and coordination of extension and intension). It
nevertheless seems a considerable achievement at this age.
Even though they are not based on the deliberate choice of a
common characteristic, the various collections are distinguished by their intrinsic qualities (of being rods, balls, or
cubes). Furthermore, though they do not have a logical extension; they are not simply new material entities in which the
elements lose their individuality, but groupings of equivalent
elements.

While the making of these collections has been represented as a continuation of the activity of filling, it is not
thought simply to be its direct descendant. The ability to make
collections of equivalent elements only becomes possible by
coordinating the activity of filling with the activities of distribution and individualization. Before considering the latter two
activities, we wish to discuss nesting, which is a special case
(i.e., putting either cubes or cups into one another).

Nesting

In all three classes of objects, the objects differ in size, yet only the cubes or cups lend themselves to nesting, and thus to behavior in which the taking into account of regular differences can easily be observed.

It has already been described how children from 10 months on, during *putting into,* try to put one cube into another and come up against the dual nature of some cubes, which can simultaneously be both container and content. From 16 months on, all the children were observed to start combining three or four cubes.

K. *at 18;13* fits C1 into C2 and puts both of them into C6. A little later, she puts C4 into C6 and presses with C6 on one of the edges of C5. She then succeeds in nesting the two pairs C1–C2 and C4–C6.

F. *at 18;14* puts C1 into C3 and presses them against one of the sides of C4. At the end of the session, F. puts C1 into C2 and presses with them against the side of C3.

S. *at 16 months* makes several attempts to nest the three smallest cubes (e.g., puts C1 into C3, tries to put C2 into C3–C1). Not succeeding, S. tries several times to get C1 out of C3, and finally succeeds by turning them over, puts C2 into C3 and tries to add C1, but without success (makes at least five attempts of this kind).

M. *at 17 months* puts C3 in C4, then takes C6 and tries to put C3–C4 into it, but does not succeed. M. takes C3 out of C4 and puts it into C6, then tries to put C4 in also, but does not succeed.

L. *at 19 months* observes C4 and puts it into C6, then takes C5, observes it and lets it go. Then L. puts C1 into C3 and tries to put C2 in also. L. soon gives up and puts C2 into C6–C4, then L. takes C1 out of C3 and puts it into C6–C4–C2.

D. *at 19 months* places C6 with the opening upwards. D. has
difficulty in inserting C5, but finally succeeds. D.
succeeds without difficulty in putting C4 into C6–C5
then takes C1 and puts it into C6–C5–C4.

In these examples, it seems that the children are not
concerned with using *all* the cubes and that they do not notice
the equality of the differences in size: When D. puts C1 into the
triplet C6–C5–C4, he does not seem to notice when C1 only
very partially fills C4, whereas the larger three are closely fitted
one into the other. If he does notice it, the observation does
not seem to suggest to him that other cubes can be inserted between C4 and C1; this type of inference is not yet
available to D.

It is precisely such an inference that is observable
indirectly in the behavior of a child who has, for example, put
C2 into C4, takes it out again, looks for and finds C3, puts it
into C4 and subsequently adds C2. This type of behavior goes
together with using all the cubes, which is certainly not
unconnected with the capacity for inference.

Complete nesting thus comprises systematic attempts
that extend to the whole collection: The attempts relate to the
equivalence of the differences in size. A variety of strategies may be
followed in order to reach the desired result.

This is how children proceed with the rounded cups:

A. *at 18 months* first puts C2 into C4, takes it out immediately
and replaces it by C3. A. adds C2 to C4–C3 and then
C1 to the others. After having taken the four cups
apart, he immediately starts nesting them again.
Without hesitating, he first puts C4 into C5; and then
one by one, he puts in C3, C2, and C1, thus
succeeding in nesting all the cups.

N. *at 24 months* puts C1 into C3, lifts up both of them and
puts them into C5. Then N. takes C4 and places it on
top of C1–C3–C5. Because C4 refuses to nest, she

takes one of the rods and beats with it on C4 (in order to make it go in?); then she takes all of them apart. After a pause, she forms pairs of cups of consecutive size: C3 into C4 and C1 into C2. Again, she undoes her work. Once more she puts C3 into C4 but takes it out immediately in order to put C4 into C5. Without hesitating, she adds C3, C2, and C1, one after the other, thus succeeding in nesting all the cups.

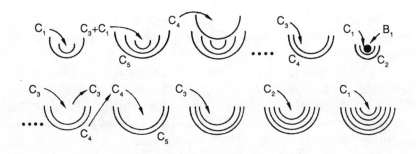

Nesting is more difficult with the cubes. For complete nesting, two different strategies were observed: assemble two triplets or assemble three pairs.
V. at 24 months uses both strategies:

Two triplets—V. nests C5 in C6, nests C4 in C6–C5, nests C2 and C1, and then puts both into C6–C5–C4 and then takes them out again. V. takes C2–C1 and puts them into C3, then nests C3–C2–C1 in C6–C5–C4.

Three pairs—V. puts C1 into C2, then C4 into C6. V. empties C5 of the clay balls it contained, takes C4 out of C6, and puts C5 into C6. Then V. puts C4 into C6–C5 and takes it out immediately. V. puts C3 into C4, then C2–C1 into C4–C3, and finally C4–C3–C2–C1 into C6–C5.

It is to be noted that in both strategies, V. takes one cube out of another several times without it being necessary; for complete nesting, the cube could have been left in place. In the second example, V. takes C4 out of the combination C6–C5–C4, where in fact C4 was in its right place, and she uses it as the container for C3, thus forming a second pair, whereupon she puts the second pair into the first and the nested quadruplet into C6–C5. These behaviors are clearly intentional, and the question arises, "For what reason, in obedience to what idea, does the child go in for actions that are useless from the point of view of the final result aimed at and in fact achieved?" This behavior may be compared with what has been noted at a much later age in the task of seriating sticks of different sizes. There also, the child makes couples and triplets for a start before being able to set up the entire series. However, the child of 4 years generally does not succeed in coordinating the couples and triplets, whereas the child of 2 years not only succeeds in nesting but also seems capable of anticipating the coordination of the whole.

We now come to a different sequence of actions. K.'s behavior at 23 months was striking because of its resemblance to behaviors typical of older children who have been asked to carry out seriation tasks. Still interested in the dual nature of the cubes as container and content, K. makes a rather exceptional demonstration: She achieves a perfect seriation of four cubes and checks each one for its dual nature of container and content.

K. at 23 months takes C4 and puts it into C6; takes C4 out of C6 and puts it aside; takes C3 and puts it into C4; takes C3 out of C4 and holds it in her right hand. With her left hand, K. takes C2 and puts it into C3 (in her right hand); with her left hand, K. takes C2 out of C3, lets go C3; with her right hand, K. takes C1 and puts into C2, which she holds in her left hand. K. protects C2–C1 with her left hand, while with her right hand she nests C3, C4, and C5.

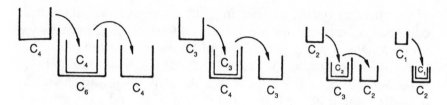

In this example, K. not only succeeds in seriating the cubes according to size but also combines it with an idea that might already be called a certain "transitivity": The cube she inserts into a larger one is taken out to become in turn the container of the cube of the next smaller size, and she does this four times in a row. Each of the four cubes used thus successively serves first as container and then as content.

Establishing Correspondences

As has been seen earlier, distribution is at first only a distribution of action (the children, in using one of the rods to touch the various members of a class, distribute their actions and individualize each member by noting its location); but now, distribution becomes coordinated little by little with putting together the members of the same class of objects, and thus it leads to creating the first couples of pairs. From 16 months on, combinations of this type become more frequent. The child creates more and more content–container pairs until at about 24 months a complete one-to-one correspondence of objects of two kinds may be achieved.

Here are some examples of this development:

F. at 18;14 puts B6 into C5, lifts up the pair, and empties B6 into C6. With his hand, F. takes B6 out of C6 and puts it into C5. F. lifts up C5–B6 and again pours B6 into C6.

It is interesting that in this example the child seems to discover the equivalence of two sequences of actions: (1) *putting into* followed by *taking out by hand* (a directly inverse action that cancels the first result) and (2) *putting into something else* (yielding a new result) and *putting into* followed by *pouring* (a combined action, part of which is the cancellation of the first action by an action of a different kind). At about the same age, distribution actions are noted with a whole series of containers, followed by the action of dropping the object into the last container. For example,

K. at 17;22 takes R6 in her right hand, sets C5 upright with her left so that the opening is upward, and puts in R6 (without letting it go). Then very rapidly, she does the same with C6, C4, C3, and then lets R6 go in C5.

This type of activity even gave rise to a unique (in our experience) event, in which a series was carried out without any content object whatever.

V. at 15;23 first puts B5 into C4. V. lifts up C4–B5, beats with it on C5, and empties it by pouring B5 into C5. V. takes B5 out of C5 and puts it into C4, then takes B5 out of C4, and lets it go. V. then continues her activities of *putting into, pouring, putting into something else* and *taking out of* without a content object. Rather absentmindedly, she puts her left hand into C4 and notices that the cube is empty. She pretends to take something from behind her and puts "it" into C4. She repeats the gesture, symbolically empties the "content" of C4 into C5, lifts up C5, and looks into it, puts her right hand into C4, takes out its "content," and puts it symbolically into C5.

This behavior of V.'s provided one of the rare occasions where a partial detachment of the action scheme becomes observable, a detachment that presages interiorization and representation.

Pairs may be created by actions other than *putting into* (i.e., by *putting in contact*, e.g., on top of, or next to, or end-to-end with). For example,

F. at 18;14 presses with R3 on B6, presses with R1 on B1. F. puts end-to-end R1 and R3, and then B1 and B2.

F. at 20;11, holding them up, establishes contact between B4 and B3, and then between B1 and B2.

In these kinds of behaviors, the child's own body may become part of the action:

K. at 16;4 puts her index finger against B1 (in midair) and then puts R6 end-to-end with B1.

These pairing activities, which all the children were observed to pursue, are soon extended to more than two members of two classes:

M. at 18 months puts B5 into C5, which he holds up. M. puts down the ball–cup pair; then he puts B3 into C4 and puts B1 into C3. He thus distributes three balls into three cups.

K. at 18;13 (C6 and C4 are nested) puts B4 into C6–C4, puts B6 into C5, puts B5 into C3 (or rather on top of C3 because B5 does not fit in).

K. at 22 months puts B1 into C4, puts B3 into C3, turns C5 upright and puts B5 into C5. K. then puts B2 into C1 (thus obtaining four cube–ball pairs).

L. at 16;22 puts B6 into C6, then B4 into C5. L. touches C3 and C4. L. takes B3, which she tries to stuff into C3 but does not succeed. L. lifts up C3 and shoves B3 into it, puts them down, takes B2 (vocalizes); shoves C4 near her other hand, and puts B2 into C4 (four ball–cube pairs, interrupted by an action indicating one by one, and apparently already with a certain seriation by size).

J. at 19;4 stirs R3 inside C4, lets it go inside, then takes it out . . . takes C5. While he is holding it up, he presses with R6 on it, takes R5 and stirs with it inside C1 (while he is holding both of them up), then takes R2 and stirs with it in C2 (also while holding them up).

P. at 20 months puts R3 into C6, then R2 into C3. P. takes R4 and R6 in his hand, lets go R6 and puts R4 into C4. P. takes up R6 again and tries to put it into C2, which is placed with the opening at the side. P. sets C2 upright and tries for a long time to put R6 into C2, does not succeed and tries to place it in C3, then does not succeed any better and lets go.

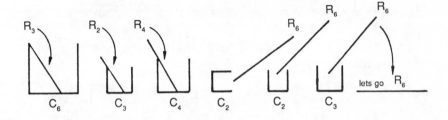

The close link between the activities here called *collecting* and *establishing correspondences* comes out clearly in the following examples:

I. at 21 months puts B4, B5, B6 into C6. I. takes out B5 and puts it into C5, which is wedged against her, then takes B4 out of C6 and also puts it into C5. Then I. does the same with B6, takes two balls simultaneously out of C5 and puts them into C4 (in front of her on the floor), then takes the third ball out of C5 and also puts it into C4. During the same session, I. also plays another game: Using different rods, she scratches successively in C6, C4, then in C5 and C2, and she finally takes R1 and scratches with it in C1.

J.P. at 23 months after having put several balls of clay into C6, takes R6 and presses with it on the balls, keeping it in his left hand. J.P. takes R2, presses with it on the balls and passes it over to his left hand, then performs the same series of actions with R3, R4, and R5,

so that in the end he has five rods in his left hand.
He then uses both hands to put the rods neatly parallel on the floor.

These two examples show how the distributing type of
activity is combined with collecting: filling is alternated with
distributing and coordinated with actions in which both differences in size and equivalences in size relations are taken into
account (choosing the smallest rod to put it into the smallest
cube, etc.).

At the age of about 24 months, several children were
observed to make complete pairings of all the members of two
classes.

This is how one child (in Tehran, using rounded cups)
reached this result:

F. *at 25 months* starts straightaway by distributing the balls
into the cups. F. puts B1 into C1, B2 into C2, B3 into
C4, B4 into C5; F. takes B5, looks at it, and puts it
down.

F. thus started his distribution by respecting the relative
sizes of the first two pairs, but his order of cups is not quite
regular, he ends up with the largest ball (B5) and a medium cup
(C3). He then continued with various efforts to adjust the balls
and cups as follows:

F. takes B1 out of C1 and puts C1 into C3 (the one that had
stayed empty), then adds B1; takes B1 out of C3–C1
and puts in B5; then he undoes all of them.

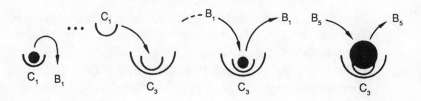

In the following attempt, he places the smallest ball successively into two empty containers of different size:

F. puts B1 into C1, takes it out and puts it into C3, takes it out and puts it back again into C1.

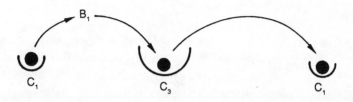

Following this attempt, in which he indeed seems to take an interest in the relative size of the cups, F. undoes all the pairs and starts a new distribution as follows:

F. puts B3 into C4, B5 into C3, B1 into C1, B2 into C2, B4 into C5. F. stops and examines the constituted pairs.

Apparently dissatisfied, he undoes the pairs B4–C5 and B5–C3, and goes on to a new adjustment of size by putting two large balls, one after the other, into C5.

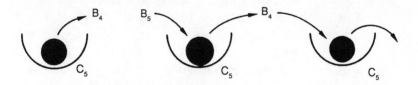

Following this attempt, he puts B5 into C5, undoes the couple B3–C4, and puts B3 into C3 (thus respecting their relative size) and finally B4 into C4.

F. thus achieved an exhaustive one-to-one correspondence of the balls and the cups by seriating step-by-step the members of the two classes according to their size. But he still did not seem satisfied with his achievement and proceeded with an activity that to us was quite unexpected: he aligned the pairs in the following order: B5–C5, B3–C3, B4–C4, B2–C2, B1–C1.

B_5 C_5 B_3 C_3 B_4 C_4 B_2 C_2 B_1 C_1

Two intermediate pairs are not placed in descending order.

The activities of three children exemplify what was observed in Paris (open cubes) when they reached the stage of establishing one-to-one correspondences.

The first example concerns K., whom we followed regularly between 12 and 14 months. K.'s quest for seriated pairs has already been presented. Observed at 24 months, she set up five pairs out of a possible six. This is how she went about it:

K. *at 24 months* takes B6 and puts it into C5, then puts B4 into C4, and then puts B5 into C6 (K. has thus made three pairs with the three largest cubes). She interrupts the making of pairs by taking up B1 and B2 at the same time and putting them into C5–B6. She plays for a while with the three smallest cubes by putting them in a row and nesting them, whereupon she takes B3 out of C6 and puts it on top of C2, then takes B2 out of C6 and puts it on top of C1. K. has thus constituted the following pairs: C5–B6, C4–B4, C6–B5, C2–B3, C1–B2. K. then goes on to do other things without having set up the sixth pair.

The second example concerns C., who was observed for the first time at the age of 24 months and had never seen the materials before. After a few minutes of various manipulations, he also achieved a one-to-one correspondence of balls and cubes:

C. *at 24 months* (there are only five balls of clay), after having touched C6 and set C2 upright, he takes B1 and puts it into C3, then takes B3 and puts it into C4, then puts B6 into C6, sets C5 upright, and puts B5 into it, then takes B2, which he puts into C2. C. takes C1, which remained empty, looks at the researcher and tries to put C1 into C2–B2 then into C3–B1, and then lets it go.

C. thus almost achieved a double seriation. The (fortuitous) absence of one of the balls (B4) created a problem for him. He clearly had expected to be able to pair off each ball with a cube. Although the increasing sizes are not quite correctly adjusted (he finished with C6–B6, C5–B5, C4–B3, C3–B1, C2–B2, with C1 empty), he clearly took relative size into account.

Particularly surprising was V.'s exploit. V. also was a child whom we saw for the first time at 24 months. She also had not handled our materials previously. When the objects were placed before her, she looked at them for a long time without touching them. (They were strewn at random, as in all our observations.) After this visual examination of the objects, in one continuous action, she achieved a corresponding arrangement of all the members of the two classes—balls and cubes.

V. at 24 months takes B3 in her right hand and B4 in her left, puts B4 into C5, then sets C6 upright and puts B3 into it. V. puts B1 into C4, and then B2 into C2. V. puts C2–B2 down right next to C6–B3 and C4–B1, takes B6 and places it on C3 (it does not go in), then puts them down in line with the other pairs. Then V. puts B5 on C1 (it does not go in), and aligns this pair also.

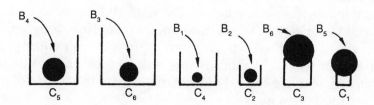

V. thus paired all the members of the ball class with all the members of the cube class. What interested her was evidently the pairing—the one-to-one correspondence—and not the spatial relationship of container–content. V. did not at all take the differences in size into account, but, as has been seen previously, she is perfectly capable of doing so, for in the same session, she made a perfect nesting. Contrary to C., who took size into account, she introduced a different element, just as F. had done (i.e., the precise alignment of the six pairs—C6–B3, C4–B1, C2–B2, C3–B6 [*on top* instead of *in*] C5–B4, C1–B5 [*on top* instead of *in*] The alignment is quite intentional and very carefully made, though certainly arrived at step by step (i.e., without a representation of the series as a whole). Nevertheless, it does not seem excessive to consider the alignment as another manifestation of the coordination between individualization and collection—it is the spatial disposition that gives a unified character to a collection made up of paired elements.

At the end of the age period ending at 24 months, we were thus able to observe a culmination of prelogical activities elicited by the materials presented, which directed the attention of the children to various iterated action sequences and to their results. At this time in their development, the children succeed in making exhaustive collections of identical objects; in constructing a seriation with cubes or cups, according to size (the first, which is the largest and will contain all the others, the next, the next, and so on); and in establishing a one-to-one correspondence (successive pairings between members of two classes of objects until all the objects have been paired).

As our observations at the different ages indicate, the activities of collecting, distributing, and nesting seem to be closely linked. During the period from 12 to 18 months, the link is apparent in the shifts from one of these activities to the other: the child makes a few pairs then becomes interested, for example, in the similarities of the rods and starts to make a collection, or puts one cup into another, replaces it by one of the balls of clay, then sets up another cup–clay pair. During the period from 18 to 24 months, the link is apparent in that the three activities are carried out exhaustively in the course of one observation session.

The relationships among the different activities (of which we have sketched the development) seem to us of particular interest due to the Piagetian epistemological analysis of the construction of number. In *Mathematical Epistemology and Psychology* (1961/1966), Piaget rejects the propositions of authors such as Russell, Whitehead, and Frege as being too restrictive, and he proposes a genesis of number arising from the synthesis of classes and relations, while attributing special importance to one-to-one correspondence.

It was found in an experiment in which the subjects put a bead into a bowl with one hand, while with the other putting a bead into a larger bowl, that there are children who do not yet succeed in the number conservation test in its classical form, but who in this experiment perceive the unlimited equality of collections: "If you know it once, you know it for ever," a 5-year-old explained as quoted by Inhelder and Piaget (Gréco et al., 1963, p. 66).

According to Inhelder and Piaget, the quotation is an early example of recursive reasoning. The precocity of the inference that leads to the conservation of equality can be explained by the kinds of actions the children were asked to perform. On the one hand, adding elements one by one leads to an *inclusion* sequence (*cardinal* value), as well as to an order that is inherent in the *temporal* succession of adding gestures (*ordinal* value). On the other hand, the action of making the correspondence involves numerical equality. In other words,

> as the child establishes a link between his successive
> actions and their results, he constructs a synthesis between
> the temporal order of his actions . . . and the gradual
> growth of the collections. . . . Thus, in the very union of
> actions and their cumulative result, the numerical synthesis
> is prefigured in a way that is practical or even motoric.
> (Gréco et al., 1963, p. 115)

It seems to us that much more primitive prefigurations appear in the behaviors we observed among our subjects at the age of 18 to 24 months. Indeed, the components of the actions that at an early age allow the complex inference of equality to be made are already present in the actions most frequently performed by the infants with the materials we placed at their disposal: adding objects one by one (collection), carrying out a spatiotemporal succession of gesture (distribution), and establishing one-to-one correspondences (the pairing of members of two classes of objects).

An Account of One 20-Minute Observation Session

The various types of activity that have been described follow one another and are repeated throughout the observation sessions. The children are fiercely persistent in trying to put into practice what they have in mind whenever the materials counteract their plans. Given the materials we proposed to the children, it was activities of collecting, nesting, and establishing correspondences that very clearly predominated.

To illustrate the scope and variety of activities in the course of an observation session, it may be worth presenting one protocol in its entirety. Here is K.'s at 24 months:

(To facilitate reading the protocol, sequences have been annotated using the following abbreviations: C = collecting, D = distributing, N = nesting, EC = establishing a correspondence, ? [question mark] = the less clearly organized activities.)

? K. holds in her left hand the two largest rods (R5 and R6), absentmindedly presses them on B6.

EC. K. starts with her right hand to distribute the balls of clay into the three cubes (B6 into C5, B4 into C4, and B5 into C6).

C. Instead of continuing the distribution, K. starts collecting balls of clay in the two largest cubes (puts B2 and B3 into C6–B5, and puts B1 into C5–B6).

? (plays with the three smallest cubes). K. puts C2 into C3 and takes it out again, grasps and lets go of C2, grasps and lets go of C1, and handles C1 and C2.

EC (returns to distribution). K. takes B4 out of C4 and puts it back in again, repeats the action twice, then takes B3 out of C6–B5–B2, and puts it on top of C2. then K. takes B2 out of the same C6–B5 and puts it on top of C1, then puts C1–B2 next to C2–B3.

EC (the correspondence K. has established is imperfect). She has made four pairs (C4–B4, C6–B5, C1–B2, and C2–B3), and she uses a fifth cube (C5), but it contains two balls (B6 and B1), and she did not use C3.

? (for a short while, her play is rather disorganized). She touches one ball with another, puts one ball into C5, scratches the outer surface of C6 and C4.

N (after having emptied C6 and C4 by turning them over, she starts nesting the cubes). K. puts C1 into C2 and then C2–C1 into C3. She takes out C3 and puts it into C4. N. passes C4–C3 from one hand to the other, takes C3 out of C4, puts it back in, and takes it out again. She covers C2–C1 first by C3, then by C4; she takes away C3 and C4, then puts C2–C1 into C4–C3 (the four smallest cubes are thus correctly nested). She then takes C1–2–3 out of C4, sets C4 aside, takes the two balls out that are still in C5, turns over and handles C5, takes the small ball out of C6, puts C5 into C6, and then puts C4 into C6–5 (she thus establishes two triplets). She then puts C3–2–1 into C6–5–4 and thus achieves a complete nesting of the six cubes.

C (immediately afterward, collects the six rods). K. holds R6 and R5 in her right hand, and R2 and R4 in her left. She passes R6 and R5 into her left hand, seizes the last two rods (R3 and R1) with her left hand, and thus has the complete collection of rods in her left hand. While still holding on to the rods, she starts handling the balls of clay, first B2 and B3, then B5; she puts down the six rods and aligns them.

C (starts collecting the balls in the nested cubes). She first puts in B2 and B3, then B4; she can just still manage to get in B5 (which goes well over the edge) then adds B6, supporting it with her hand because otherwise it would fall down (B1 is hidden under her leg). Five balls are now collected in the cubes. She proceeds to take out the balls: B6 and B5 with her left hand, then B4 and B3 with her right, then B1 with her right hand, and she puts down the three balls while holding B6 and B5 in her left hand.

N (sets about disassemblng the cubes). K. takes out C3–2–1 (with B2 still inside), turns them over, but nothing comes out. K. puts down the balls in her left hand, takes the three small nested cubes and turns them over in her right hand. C2–C1–B2 fall into her right hand. She puts down C3, lifts up C2, tosses it away. While holding on to B2 in her right hand, K. puts C1 into C3, takes up C2 again and puts it into C3–C1, turns them over (the cubes are emptied), puts down C3, puts C2 into C3, and then C1 into C3–2 (she has renested the three smallest cubes).

? (for a short while, she indulges in a mixture of activities with the balls). She lifts them up and passes them from one hand to the other. While she is doing this, B4 falls on the three little nested cubes.

Construction. K. tries to add another ball on top of B4, but the construction collapses and the three nested cubes come apart.

Transformation. K. starts plucking bits from B4, puts B4 into C6–5–4, then takes some bits from B3, which she also puts into C6–C5–C4–B4. She takes other balls in her hands, but puts them down without plucking at them. (After an interruption, all the cubes are empty and set on the floor.)

D. K. turns over all the cubes so that the opening is at the bottom (C3, C1, C2, and C5) except C6 and C2, which are already in that position. Then, after having placed a large ball (B6) on C6, K. uses R6, which she holds in her right hand, to touch the patterns on some of the cubes—C5, C4, C3, and again C4.

EC (comes back to correspondences). She turns over C5 and puts R6 into it, takes R5 and with it touches one of the patterns on C3, then turns over C3 and puts R5 into it, turns over C1 and C2 and puts R2 and R1 into them, turns over C4 and puts R3 into it and then R4 (because B6 is on C6).

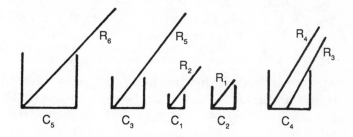

C. (collects all the rods in C4). She takes R5 out of C3 and puts it into C4, which already contains R3 and R4. She takes R6 out of C5 and puts it into C4–B4–B5, then takes B1 and B2 out of C2 and C1, and puts them also into C4–B3–B4–B5–B6.

C. (again makes a collection of all the six rods). K. takes them one by one out of C4 and putting them into C5.

EC. (starts making a new correspondence using the balls). She puts B5 on C3, and then B4 on C1, unsticks B3 from B2, plucks some pieces off B2, and then puts it into C4 (there are thus three pairs).

C. K. turns C4 over and puts in B2, takes four rods out of C5 and puts them down, takes the last two rods out of C5 and puts them into C4–B2, and then adds three other rods (B6 remains outside the collection).

EC. (Having upset the pair C1–B2 with her foot, again takes up the correspondence of balls and cubes). B5 is already on C3. She puts B4 back on C1 and puts B3 on C2; she aligns the three pairs.

? K. takes the five rods out of C4–B2 and puts in B1, then takes B6 out of C6, turns C6 over and puts in B6, places C6–B6 on C5. She takes out C6–B6 and sets it down, puts C5 into C6–B6, then takes C5 and then B6 out of C6.

N (proceeds to nest the cubes). K. puts C5 into C6, takes B2 and B1 out of C4, puts C4 into C6–5, puts B1 into C6–5–4, puts C3 into C6–5–4–B1, then adds C2, takes B4 out of C1 and puts it into C6–5–4–B1–C2, then takes it out again and puts in C1 instead, puts B4 on top, adds B6, takes out B4 and then B6 from C6–5–4–B1–C3–2–1.

C. (collects the six rods in her left hand). K. takes R3 in her right hand, and R2 and R4 in her left, passing R3 to her left hand and seizing the last three rods with her left hand.

? K. takes B6 and B4 in her right hand, loses B6, puts B4 into C6–C5–C4–B1–C3–C2–C1, takes it out, puts it in her left hand, loses it, takes it up again with her right hand, then plays for a while at rolling B6 on her leg.

C. (K. continues to play with the rods.) She passes the six rods from her left hand to her right and then passes them one by one to her left hand, keeping only R6 in her right hand; touches the other rods with R6, puts R6 end-to-end with R1, puts R6 back with the other rods. She passes all the rods to her right hand and lets them go, except for R6. She touches the extremity of R6 with her left hand, then presses her belly with R6. She again touches the extremity of R6, then presses R6 on her thigh, passes R6 to her left hand and touches the extremity of R6 with her right hand. She again presses it against her thigh, then takes the other five rods in her left hand.

Spatial. K. aligns the balls of clay in the space between her
legs, ? loses the rods, touches the balls, sticks B3 onto
one of the other balls, takes some of the rods and
starts pressing with them on the clay balls.

Summary and Conclusions

By making available to children aged 10 to 24 months several
objects they were not familiar with (open cubes or cups,
wooden rods, and balls of modeling clay—six of each object
class, with regular differences in size), we were able to observe
a progressive organization of prelogical behaviors such as
collecting, nesting, and establishing correspondences.

At the age of 10 months (the start of our observations),
children already showed differentiated actions, according to
the different properties of the objects: The rods were more
frequently used for tapping, the cubes gave rise to explorations
of exterior and interior surfaces, and the balls of modeling clay
elicited actions such as pressing on them, biting them, and so
on. At the same time, children engaged in repetitive actions on
different members of the same class of objects, such as touching several cubes one after the other.

One or 2 months later, (11–12 months of age), with the
same objects, a new form of behavior emerged and remained
predominant for a considerable time (i.e., putting one object
inside another). This activity enabled the child progressively to
grasp the container–content relationship as well as the specific
shape and the graduated size of the objects.

With all the children observed, the action of *putting into*
was followed immediately by taking the content-object out
again. This new combination of actions both (a) enabled
children to realize that an action can cancel the effect of
a previous action and (b) helped them to understand the
container–content properties of the objects at their disposal.

At the age of about 12 to 13 months, the children were
observed to perform the first sequences that take the form of

iterative actions. These follow two directions: (1) putting to-gether and (2) distributing. At the age of about 24 months, the reciprocal organization of these two types of activity leads to setting up one-to-one correspondences of the members of two classes of objects.

Two Periods of Prelogical Organization

Two periods can be distinguished in this progressive organization: before and after 16 to 18 months. A qualitative change occurs at this watershed age, bringing about a kind of rupture in the progressive structuration of prelogical behaviors.

The Earlier Period (12 to 16–18 Months)

During this time, the child largely either accumulates dissimilar objects or performs actions that may be called distributions, which seem to individualize and localize the objects.

When accumulating, the children gather objects in one of the two largest cubes. The aim seems to be simply to fill, because they do not choose any specific class of content-objects, choosing instead simply any objects that are small enough. The large cube becomes the first collection point. As in an even earlier period, when it was simply a matter of *putting into*, the child still empties the filled receptacle immediately afterward, and the emptying is still done by hand, one object after the other.

Behaviors that announce distribution make their appearance during this same period. The same action (almost always using one of the rods) is repeated on several objects of the same class (e.g., stirring with the stick in several cubes). In this way, the child seems to individualize and to localize the various objects. It is a kind of sketchy identification of similar objects.

From this age on, the children combine two kinds of activity: They may either (1) remove the content from one container and put it into another container (container substitution) or (2) replace the content-object with another object (content substitution). At this time, the first coupled pairs of two containers and two content-objects of the same class make their appearance.

The Later Period (16–18 to 24 Months)

The behaviors that were observed in this later period did not fail to surprise us: The children proceeded spontaneously (without anyone having suggested it to them) to impose a logical organization on the objects by collecting, nesting, and establishing correspondences.

Collecting   Contrary to the preceding period (when the children filled the cubes), in this new period, they worked toward the aim of putting together what belongs together. They chose objects of the same class and put them together in the same place, which was not necessarily in a cube, but which may, for example, have been between their legs, in a place on the floor. For *putting together*, they no longer need a receptacle (hand, cube).

Nesting   To be able to nest the series of six cubes, children needed to solve the problem of the equivalent differences in size. While at first they did not seem to be concerned by the absence of one or two cubes in the nested series, we observed children at the age of about 24 months using two methods in order to nest the whole series—either two triplets or three pairs were formed before the complete series was nested.

Establishing One-to-One Correspondences   More and more frequently and in increasingly varied ways, the children began to combine two kinds of actions (i.e., putting together and distributing). This led to the establishment of increasingly numerous pairs belonging to two different classes of objects (most frequently a container and a content object). Finally, at the age of about 24 months, the child created some exhaustive sets of pairs of objects of two classes. The point seemed to be the pairing, for some children who were engaged in this activity neglected the container–content relationship and did not seem to be bothered by a ball of modeling clay being too big to go into the cube with which it was being paired. Clearly, this is a form of abstraction: The objects are no longer considered for their physical properties but are dealt with as equivalent elements belonging to a certain class. This is clearly an early step toward the idea of objects as devoid of all properties except cardinal or ordinal values.

Importance of This Organization

What are the most important aspects of this spectacular organization of behaviors? In the first place, it should be underlined that between 12 and 24 months, the prelogical behaviors described cover almost all the activities observed during each session.

The children showed great tenacity in organizing the materials at their disposal in more and more complex ways: Once they had started pursuing an idea, they started again, they tried once more a little differently, and they did not tire of trying.

As we had hoped, the proffered materials favored a specific direction for the child's efforts and led to certain types of activities rather than others. What we did not expect was the coherence and the fruitfulness of this progressive structuration.

We have called these activities "prelogical." The root, *logical,* is used because the children, at a very early age, allowed us to observe constructions that are similar to those Piaget pointed out as indicating a logicomathematical organization of the concrete operational period. In its ordinary sense, the prefix *pre-* simply indicates that these activities make their appearance well before the truly logical operations of the 6–8-year-olds. More fundamentally, we consider these activities as preceding and preparing for later logicomathematical reasoning. In particular, we observed prelogical behaviors that strikingly illustrate the parallelism between the development of class inclusion, seriation, and whole numbers. According to Piaget, whole numbers are to be regarded as a new construct based on the synthesis of class inclusion and seriation and supported by one-to-one correspondence; the latter provides the subject with a construction procedure that leads to a reference system through recursive reasoning. The connections, no doubt very complex, between the activities observed in this research and the nascent structuration of the various logical operations brought to light by Piaget remain to be studied.

In the course of the present research, we also, though not frequently, observed behaviors relevant to spatiotemporal organization and to causal reasoning. Further research is needed with materials more appropriate for the purpose of exploring structuration in these domains during the same period. However, in our opinion, the different kinds of materials incite the children to different focuses of interest and thus facilitate the observer's task of describing development in the various domains of knowledge that have been distinguished by epistemologists. We do not consider that the different experimental situations bring to light totally different capacities (linked only by their existence within the same subject). On the contrary, the various capacities brought to light in the different situations are functionally linked, and each particular one is the expression of a unitary structure—certainly in subjects as young as ours.

Two outstanding features of this research are the very early appearance of (1) complex behaviors by which the children both organize their reasoning and organize reality, and, above all, (2) the tenacious interest with which they pursue the solution of the problems they set themselves.

CHAPTER 2

Infants and Physics

S. Rayna, H. Sinclair, and M. Stambak

The preceding chapter analyzed prelogical activities of children aged 10 to 24 months. During that research, we occasionally observed activities such as taking a ball of modeling clay to bits, throwing it, or trying to balance a rod on a cup. These behaviors indicated that the child's focus of attention was not as much on the actions and their coordination as on the objects and their properties. We then decided to study more closely this physical object-oriented aspect of the children's behavior. What are the questions the children ask themselves about the objects, and how do they go about answering them? That is the theme of this second chapter.

Method

Again, not wanting to encroach upon the children's activities, we created a situation similar to the one described in the preceding chapter: The children were filmed while freely interacting with a collection of objects in the presence of an observer who showed interest in their activities but who did not interfere. The observation sessions, which were held in the rooms of the day-care center the children were accustomed to, lasted about 20 minutes.

Materials

We presented the children with numerous, small, unfamiliar objects having varied properties, placed pellmell on the floor: a tube, beads, paper balls, string, cardboard, a metal grid, cubes, a piece of cloth, a pipe cleaner, cotton balls, polystyrene chips,[1]

---

[1] Bits of polystyrene plastic that can be picked apart.

a wooden board, a larger and a smaller stick, two rubber bands, a sheet of paper, uncooked spaghetti noodles, and a ball of modeling clay.

Population

A total of 45 observations were made, 18 of them cross-sectional and 27 semilongitudinal (see Tables 2.1 and 2.2).[2]

At the same ages, no differences in behavior types were observed between the children who used the materials only once and those who used them several times.

Condensation of the Observation Protocols

As in the research described in the preceding chapter, we made detailed transcriptions of the films and analyzed the action sequences.

The Earliest Organized Actions

As noted before, children who are less than 12 months old apply their principal action patterns indifferently to any object they grasp—turning things this way and that; feeling, pressing, scratching, shaking, and putting things into the mouth; and so on. Little by little, more systematic explorations relate more closely to the properties of the objects. These early action sequences have been described in the preceding chapter, and they consist either of the same actions applied to different objects, or of a series of different actions applied to the same object. These behaviors were observed principally among children between 9 and 12 months of age.

The youngest children in the present research were also observed to carry out these early exploratory behaviors at the

---

[2] Because the young children frequently put some of the small objects into their mouth, we abandoned research with children below the age of 12 months.

Table 2.1
Cross-sectional Observations

Age in months:	11/12	13	14	15	16	17	18	19	20	21	22	23	24	25	26
Number of children:	3	1	1	2	1	1	2	—	—	1	1	2	1	—	2

Table 2.2
Longitudinal Observations

Age in months:	11/12	13	14	15	16	17	18	19	20	21	22	23	24	25	26
S.	+	+	+	+	+										
L.	+	+	+	+	+	+	+								
N.							+	+	+	+	+	+			
Sa.							+	+	+	+	+				
E.													+	+	+
K.													+	+	+

beginning of the session, when they first came in contact with the new materials. Here are some examples:

N. at 12;25, as soon as he is installed in front of the
materials, seizes the ball of clay, observes it, shows it
to the researcher, observes it afresh by turning it a
little, then puts it down where he found it. Next, he
takes a ball of paper, observes it, shows it, feels it,
brings it to his mouth, shows it again, puts it back
into his mouth, and lets it go. Next, he takes a large
conical bead, looks at its base, shows it, then puts it
aside. Next, he takes a chip, puts it into his mouth
and then gives it to the researcher. Then he takes the
bead again, puts it in his mouth, gives it to the
researcher, and so on.

In this example, roughly the same actions are applied to a variety of different objects.

T. at 12;14 takes a tube in one hand and with the other
touches the extremity of the tube. She lifts it up with
both hands and looks at it attentively. Her eyes
slowly follow the length of the tube, first in one
direction, then in the other.

S. at 11;20, after having handled various objects (stick, tube,
grid, chip), gets hold of the cardboard with one hand,
looks at it, takes it in both hands and attentively
examines both sides, turning it over several times.

N. at 12;25 takes hold of the small stick, passes it from one
hand to the other, then explores one part of it with
his index finger. Holding the stick at its extremities,
he explores different sections simultaneously with
both index fingers.

In these three examples, different actions are applied to the same object as if the better to determine its properties.
After the age of 12 months, the children's manipu-

lations become more definite and are diversified more specifically according to the objects. With the objects used in the present research, the children get to know some of their characteristics better and better as a result of detailed and prolonged explorations. They also transform the objects and succeed in combining them in various ways. In fact, after the first contacts with the objects, the activities follow two directions: transforming activities and combining activities. *Transforming activities* are carried out on a single object. It may be a matter of *fragmentation* (of objects that lend themselves easily to this activity) or *shape changing* (of objects that are not easily fragmented). When *combining* objects, the children create relationships of proximity or of envelopment.

Transforming

From the age of 12 months, the children often explore the objects for a long time. During these explorations, they realize that some of the objects are transformable: The substance of which they are composed lends itself either to fragmentation or to shape changing.

Fragmentation

The following examples will illustrate how the fragmentation activities evolve. For a start, here is how a child of about 12 months went about it:

S. *at 11;20*—a cotton ball happens to adhere to the end of the tube and attracts S.'s attention when she picks up the tube. She takes the cotton ball in both hands, feels it, looks at it, stretches it, and tears off a bit.

Very rapidly, S. discovers the possibility of pulling the cotton ball to bits. A little later in the same session, she takes the cotton ball up again and once more proceeds to shred it:

S. pulls out numerous bits of the cotton ball one after the
other until the ball is used up. She looks intensively
at the stretching of the cotton and the detachment of
the bits, which she systematically sticks together
again by pressing them hard so that they will really
hold. S., at one point, shows signs of being angry
when the bits are too compressed and no longer
adhere sufficiently. When the ball of cotton is
reconstituted with all the bits sticking together, she
pulls it apart again.

The following points stand out:

- The ball of cotton is completely pulled to bits.

- S. is very attentive to the deformation and the
  separation: She stretches the cotton very slowly and
  observes the gradual change in shape. Her interest
  seems to be centered on the point at which a bit
  separates from the rest.

- S. also performs the inverse action and puts all the
  pieces together again.

This example is fairly representative of behavior at 12
months: After observing and feeling the cotton ball, all the
infants observed soon pulled it apart.

During this fragmentation, the children are interested
in the properties of the cotton (soft, stretchable, etc.).
However, in the long process of pulling it apart and reconstituting the ball, interest seems also to be focused on the action
itself, with its prelogical characteristics as noted in the
preceding chapter: The act is repeated until the material is
exhausted and then the result is cancelled by an inverse action.

It should be added that, at 12 months, fragmenting is
observed only with objects that lend themselves easily to this
kind of transformation. This is particularly true of the cotton
wool, the fragmentability of which is spotted immediately;
attempts with other objects (e.g., the modeling clay) are rare
and do not last long.

What happens in the following months? At the age of about 15 months, fragmenting still takes first place among transformational activities, and a new feature is added: The children no longer fragment various objects in an exclusively repetitive manner, but they also do it in a recursive way—that is, the same action (cutting, tearing, etc.) is applied to the product of the following action.

Here are two typical examples of children at this age:

C. at 14;10, during the whole session, is very busy
    fragmenting things into bits. First of all, she attacks
    the modeling clay. Taking the ball of clay, she looks
    at it, feels it, then scratches it and soon detaches a
    small piece. Several times, she starts again and
    carefully looks at the pieces at the end of her finger
    and at the ball from which they were taken.

A little later, in the course of the same session, C. becomes interested in the ball of cotton:

The very moment she seizes the ball, she pulls it into two
    parts. She lets one half drop between her legs and
    immediately pulls the remainder in two, whereupon
    she drops one half next to her. She continues halving
    a number of times until there is only a tiny bit of
    cotton left, which she gets rid of by brushing her
    hands against each other.

The activity may be called "recursive." C. divides in two a piece of cotton, which itself is the result of a previous division, etc. Contrary to the 12 month-old, the pieces are no longer dropped indiscriminately but are placed in a definite spot with reference to the child's body.

After having collected the bits of cotton and put them in a
    heap, C. tears off new pieces, which she drops first
    on one side, then on the other, then between her
    legs. Finally, she divides the largest piece (the first

one to be dropped) several times. Picking up again one of the pieces, she caresses her chin with it.

From now on, the placing of the detached pieces is increasingly systematic within the spaces created by the child's own body. There may also be some interest in equalizing the size of the pieces. At the end of this example, C. demonstrated that she had discovered the softness of the cotton, which thus was no longer just something to be torn to bits but also something with special tactile qualities. Is there a suggestion here of toilet activities (cotton balls are actually used in the cleaning of a baby's nose, ears, and face in general)?

Taking up a pile of detached pieces again, C. starts pulling them further to bits and puts some of the new bits into the hand of the researcher, others between her legs, and the remainder on the side. Then she uses pieces or tears off others to caress various parts of her face for a long time (or perhaps to give herself a "moustache"). She tears up these bits still further to again caress her face with the new smaller bits.

It seems that at this point the fragmentation of the cotton ball is no longer as interesting in itself. C. seems to be checking that each little bit of cotton she has detached still is cotton (i.e., just as soft as the original piece). The way she uses it to caress her face and to "wash" herself suggests symbolic play.

To sum up, C. elaborately fragments the cotton ball. In addition to repetitive actions (tear off one bit, then another one, then another one), recursive actions were observed (tear off a large bit, then pull the large bit into two, and so on). When fragmenting, the child seems to want to make sure that the bits preserve the same qualities, the same consistency as the original whole. The interest in placing the bits and pieces in reference to the child's own body is new, not having been observed in fragmenting behavior at earlier sessions. The use of cotton in a beginning of symbolic play is also to be noted.

In the following example, a child who is preoccupied with fragmentation makes use of an unforeseen event—the accidental breaking of a stick of spaghetti—and integrates it into his previous activities.

R. at 15 months is busy tearing off bits of modeling clay. Looking for a lost piece of clay, he comes across the piece of spaghetti. He seizes it straightaway and presses with it on the floor (as the children often do with a stick). Under the pressure, the spaghetti breaks. A little later, he picks up the longest stick of spaghetti and presses with it on the floor as he had done before—once again, the spaghetti breaks. He does it three times over until the spaghetti bits are too small to be broken any further. Then he looks through the materials to find something suitable for continuing this activity. He chooses the little plastic stick (a long object with about the same diameter as the spaghetti) and tries to break it in the way he broke the spaghetti, but he does not succeed. He also tries, but in a less obvious way, to do the same thing with the pipe cleaner. During the same session, R. crumples the sheet of paper, then stretches it out again and tears it into bits until all the paper is used up.

As indicated by the examples, among the fragmentable objects, cotton balls remain the favorite for infants until about 15 months of age. In addition to the pleasure they obviously take in the activity of pulling it apart, the bits are also interesting for further playful acts.

It was also noted that children at this age tear several objects to bits, one after the other. This generalization of the activity may indicate a desire to find similarities among the objects. Varying the action—that is, the simple repetitive as opposed to the recursive method—is clearly another point of interest.

From 18 months on, fragmenting is still frequent, though it is often combined with other activities, notably in making new objects. At the same time, another transformational activity on a single object appears—that is, deformation of shape changing without fragmentation.

Around 18 months, fragmentation is at its peak. Very long sequences can be observed (e.g., Sa. at 17;24 spent 5 minutes pulling a ball of cotton to pieces; so does N. at 19 months). The ball of cotton is torn to bits, the bits are stuck together again, the reconstituted ball is once again pulled to bits, and so on. As in previous examples, the children touch their face with the bits of cotton. Gradually, this activity becomes more systematic—the children rub or caress their faces with each new piece that is torn out. In this way, the children apparently make sure that each new little bit, however small, still has the quality of being soft.

Continuing the generalizations noted at 15 months, fragmenting is now extended to more resistant objects: the ball of modeling clay, the chip, the paper ball, and the spaghetti. All but the ball of clay are completely pulled to bits.

Though the spread of this activity to many objects does not in itself introduce anything very new, there is nevertheless the beginning of a new behavior that seems to result from the resistance of certain objects to fragmenting. For example, when the children find it difficult to fragment the modeling clay by hand, they may take the stick or the tube and try to use it as an instrument for fragmentation. But because at this age the use of a tool for purposes of fragmenting is still too difficult, the attempt is rapidly abandoned, and the children return to fragmenting with their hands.

At about 24 months, by contrast, the use of certain objects as instruments in order to break apart resistant objects becomes more and more frequent. The child then seems more interested in using the instrument than in the actual fragmenting. At this age, in fact, fragmenting alone does not seem to offer sufficient interest, except sometimes during the fragmentation of great numbers of almost invisible portions of an object that is difficult to take apart (chip, balls of paper). By the age of about 24 months, fragmenting is usually a prop for other activities.

For example, N. at 23;9 or E. at 24;22 take hold of a little stick and introduce it into the cotton ball or the polystyrene chip, which up to that point they had been shredding. Then, instead of pursuing the shredding with the instrument, they use the bits they had made for activities that we have called "fabrication" (to be discussed later).

It even happens (e.g., K. at 25;4) that the children tear an object into bits in advance that they will later need for making a new object.

Shape-changing

From the age of 18 months on, activities on a single object other than fragmentation were observed. Because these activities change the shape of certain objects, they are here called "deformations." The objects that were most often "deformed" were the string and rubber band. The ball of modeling clay was not used in this way, probably because the clay was hard to kneed. The string and the rubber band held no interest for children under 18 months old, possibly because of their lack of substance. For the same reason, these two objects are seldom explored in relationship to particular parts of the body (mouth, neck, arms, feet).

An early example of exploring the rubber band follows:

L. at 17;3 (who has already used the big rubber band as a
   wraparound), in the middle of the session, takes hold
   of the big rubber band, puts her two hands inside,
   and then gently stretches it several times. She slips it
   onto her arm, but removes it straightaway and again
   stretches it with her two hands. She repeats the
   action several times with great energy.

By increasing and decreasing the tension of the band

several times, L. is apparently experiencing its elasticity with her hands. Her mouth may also play a part:

L. slips the rubber band onto her arm and then introduces her other arm into the loop from the other side. The band is now round both her arms and crosses between them, making an 8. She opens up her arms a little and raises the band to her mouth, whereupon she bites and pulls it with her teeth at the point where it crosses. After withdrawing her arms one after the other, she keeps the rubber band in her mouth and continues to chew it. Then she takes it from her mouth and again stretches it between her two hands. She again brings it to her mouth and takes hold of the part nearest to it with her teeth.

There follows yet another variation:

L. releases the tension in the rubber band and brings together the opposite sides. L. now holds the band vertically to form two loops. With her teeth, she takes hold of the upper loop, and with her hand, pulls the band away from her. Then she places it on the grid, where it surrounds a paper ball contained in one of the divisions. Throughout, L. seems to pay great attention to the changes of shape she brings about.

At the age of about 24 months, shape-changing activities with the rubber band and the string become increasingly elaborate.

Sa. at 22;7 takes the larger rubber band in both hands and stretches it several times in rapid succession. She pulls strongly on the rubber band and then reduces the tension while intensely watching its reactions.

While exploring the tensing and relaxing of the rubber band, is she also aware of the changes in shape?

Holding the rubber band in one hand, she shows it to the
   researcher, letting it dangle and at the same time
   looking at it very carefully. She then slips in her other
   hand and passes the band up to her shoulder. She
   removes the band and then stretches it again slightly,
   using both hands. She takes one hand out of the
   loop, then substitutes the other hand. For a moment,
   she again lets the band dangle and then again passes
   it up to her shoulder. She then stretches it a little by
   pulling on it with her other hand.

   After having examined the rubber band dangling from
the tip of her fingers, Sa. slips it onto her body, using one arm
after another, and in the end, she combines this activity with
stretching the band. As she continues her activities, she
becomes interested in the movements of the band when she
holds it up in the air.

Sa. takes the rubber band off her arm while vocalizing.
   Holding up the band with two hands, she examines it
   afresh. (The loop at this moment is almost circular. Is
   that what intrigues her?) Letting go with one hand,
   she continues to look at it. (the shape is now more
   oval, and the band swings a little to and fro.)
   Noticing this slight movement, she starts shaking the
   band a little and looks very closely at what happens
   while punctuating the movements with "pta . . . pta
   . . . pta. . . ." Gradually, she increases the
   movement and then stops while observing the
   reaction of the band, which continues to move for a
   second or so after she has stopped. She still says "pta
   . . . pta. . . ." She then folds the rubber band,
   makes a ball of it, stretches it once again, looks at it
   again while holding it up and humming to herself.

Almost immediately afterward she picks up the band with
   finger and thumb and looks at it closely saying "pa
   . . . pa. . . ." She then stretches it with both hands.

Next, holding it only with one hand, she keeps it in the air and observes it continuously. Rhythmically, she keeps on saying "pa . . . pa . . .; pa . . ." while waving the band gently. (At one moment, it touches her foot.) All of a sudden, she starts slipping the band onto her right foot. She tries to get in her other foot, but the band sticks between her toes, so she takes it off. She then again takes up her examination of the band held up, again with rhythmic "pa . . . pa . . . pa. . . ." Then she takes it in two hands and tries to put her head through it. In the end, she just stretches it in front of her eyes. Then she slips it over her arm and raises her arm to make the band slide to her shoulder. In that position, she stretches and relaxes the band several times before letting it go.

Sa. shows great concentration during all these activities, and throughout, she remained almost motionless except when swinging the rubber band. Similar interest in the elastic properties of objects are occasionally encountered with other children, but it is not frequent, and the sequences are much shorter (e.g., when watching the ball of clay bounce and roll about).

With children aged 18 months and over, activities similar to those described with the rubber band are pursued with the piece of string. The string, like the elastic, lacks substance, but it differs from the elastic in that it offers a greater variety of possible uses and is therefore more like one of the sticks or a piece of spaghetti.

Under the age of 18 months, very few children explore the string. Before describing the problems encountered when they do start using the string, some observations on younger children with the tube or one of the sticks may be relevant. Categorizing the tube, the stick, and the string in the same class may be justified because one of the children was seen to carry out the same action with the tube and then with the string. (At 15 months, Ch. took the tube and, holding it at both ends, brought it to his mouth and nibbled at it; this mouthing was immediately repeated with the string held horizontally.)

Another child of 15 months was observed to carry out the same action with the larger stick held horizontally.

In the following example, a child of 18 months explored the string along similar lines:

S. *at 17;24* encounters the material for the first time, and soon after the beginning of the observation session, she takes up the string. S. takes hold of the piece of string with one hand and, holding it up, examines it closely. With the other hand, she gets hold of the other end and tries to stretch the string. She does not succeed because the string is rather long and her arms are short. So she moves one of her hands toward the middle of the string, letting a large length dangle down. This time, she succeeds in stretching the string by opening her arms. She observes the stretched string and brings her face close to it.

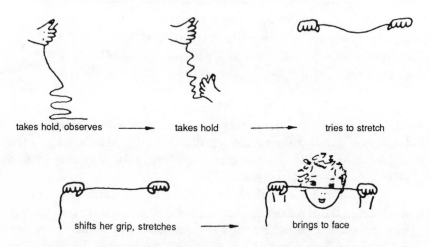

takes hold, observes ⟶ takes hold ⟶ tries to stretch

shifts her grip, stretches ⟶ brings to face

It is rather surprising to see S. correcting her grip on the string to be able to stretch it. The continuation shows that she takes the preceding results into account.

S. holds the string at the same two places and brings her hands together. She has lost the string from the hand with which she was holding the end of the string, so she takes hold of the other end of the string, brings it near her other hand which is holding the middle of the string, and then pulls her arms apart (the string is stretched). Keeping it stretched, she raises it up and

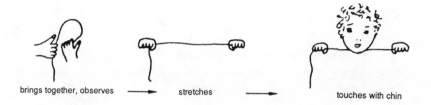

brings together, observes   ⟶   stretches   ⟶   touches with chin

touches it with her chin. After having stretched the string once more, S. raises it up, passes it over her head and around her neck while still holding it as before. She then brings her hands together and observes them carefully (the string is around her neck.) She next separates her hands, pulls slightly on the long end of the string, brings her hands together again at the same height as before. (Throughout, she is observing carefully.)

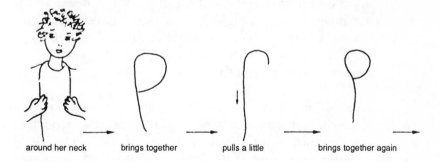

around her neck   brings together   pulls a little   brings together again

Her next actions seem to be aimed at getting rid of the string:

S. pulls on the shorter end of the string, then on the other and repeats until eventually she is rid of the string.

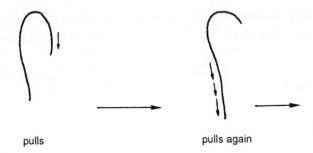

pulls   pulls again

It seems that she rapidly learns how to get rid of the string. Does she realize that when she pulls on one end, the other one goes up, and vice versa?

> She takes the string in the same way, with one hand holding about one third of the string away from the other end. She again puts it around her neck and pulls on one side and then on the other as if checking her discovery. Next, she brings her hands together and with one hand holds the string, thus making a loop. Next, she again pulls on one side and then on the other. She then lifts the string from her neck and folds it several times, making loops. With two hands, she raises up the string, stretches it, and touches the middle of it with her mouth, her chin, her neck, and her nose. Lifting it higher, she again passes it around her neck, brings the two points of manual contact together, leaves the string around her neck and proceeds to explore other objects.

In this long and systematic sequence, S. explores the continuous character of the string and brings the stretched string into contact with different parts of her body, as if marking particular points on the string. There is a suggestion of discovery of symmetry, of a midpoint, and of measurement of length.

To sum up, *fragmentation* is performed mainly on the cotton ball, the polystyrene chip, and the modeling clay. The two ways of proceeding used by the children—the iterative and the recursive—suggest a double focus of attention:

1. Focus on the properties of the objects, with each part having the same characteristics as the whole and as the other parts

2. Focus on the prelogical organization of the actions themselves, by obtaining the same result via two different procedures (i.e., the iterative and the recursive).

Shape-changing is performed on objects that have fewer than three dimensions (i.e., the rubber band and the string). Bringing them into contact with various parts of the body suggests at times a kind of marking of possible division points on an object that cannot be fragmented. The suggestion that this is an early form of measurement is taken up in a later section on threading.

Putting Things Together: Contiguity and Envelopment

At about 12 months of age, children start putting one thing in, on, or next to another. As pointed out in the preceding chapter, the children's preferred actions are to put one thing into another, but for this purpose, they must have suitable container objects. In the present collection of objects, only a few with holes lend themselves to having other objects "put into" them (e.g., the beads and the tube), and even then, the kind of "threading" that must be done is more difficult than simply putting things into open cubes or bowls.

Two examples of 12-month-old behavior (A. at 11;25 and L. at 12;4) illustrate how children start combining different objects.

A. *at 11;25* (after familarizing himself with the material via a series of usual actions) quickly goes about exploring certain striking features of the objects. For a long time, he examines the solid cube, turning it round and round in his hands and looking at every side of it. Then he looks at and feels the conical bead. Then he takes the ball of cotton and places it next to the bead. He makes a fresh start by exchanging the cotton ball for a chip. Next (taking up the cube again), he puts the bead on top of it and presses down firmly (the bead rolls and falls off the cube).

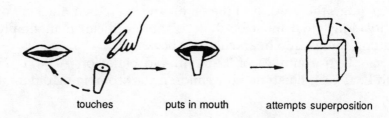

turns, observes   feels, observes   puts next to   puts next to   attempts superposition

Did he spot the flat faces of the cube and the cone in his preliminary examination? Did this suggest to him the possibility of putting one on the other? Whatever the answers, he again examined the conical bead, possibly in order to understand his failure.

He starts to bring the bead to his mouth and notices the hole in the base, which he proceeds to explore with his finger, whereupon he puts the bead in his mouth. Next, he puts it on the cube (with the short end downwards) and fails to balance it (the cone falls once again).

touches   puts in mouth   attempts superposition

As noted with many other children, A. brings the bead back to his mouth following a failure and prior to a fresh attempt at superposition.

The bead rolls away toward another object (which, as it
     happens, also has a hole)—the tube. A. takes hold of
     it, briefly brings it close to the cube, explores one of
     the ends with his finger, then presses down with it
     on the cardboard. With his free hand, he then takes
     the cube and touches one face of it and then another
     with the tube. Letting go the tube, he takes the
     conical bead and briefly holds it in line with the tube.

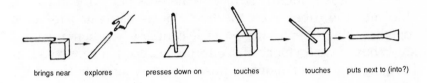

brings near   explores   presses down on   touches   touches   puts next to (into?)

With the tube, A. makes a series of rapid movements
during which the *in, on,* and *next to* relations with other objects
cannot be clearly distinguished. He then replaces the tube with
a stick, with which he tries out different spatial combinations.

A. picks up the stick, explores one end with his finger, then
     holds it vertical with one end resting on the floor.
     Next, he beats/rubs the stick on one of the sides of
     the cube (which he holds in his other hand), then on
     the top of the cube. He again explores one of the
     extremities of the stick.

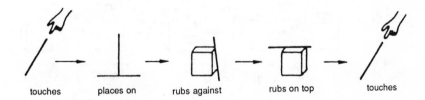

touches   places on   rubs against   rubs on top   touches

Next, A. takes a chip, looks at it, and lets it go. (It happens
     to fall just in front of the opening of the tube.) He
     immediately picks it up again and shoves it toward
     the opening. Not succeeding in introducing the chip
     into the tube, he takes hold of the tube with his other

hand and tries hard to push the chip in, first at one end of the tube, then at the other.

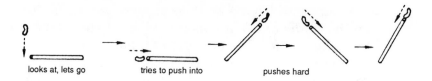

looks at, lets go   tries to push into   pushes hard

A. was evidently struck by the possibility of getting the chip into the tube when the two objects happened to come together. He perceives the possible container–content relationship; but despite tenacious efforts, he does not succeed in bringing it about. Following this failure, he again takes up his attempts at superposition.

He puts the chip on the cube (which is on the floor), but the chip slips. He tries again, but fails. Soon afterwards, he takes up the conical bead again and puts it on the cube. Having at last succeeded, he tries to lift up his construction, but it falls apart. He then tries to put the bead on top of the cube while holding them up, and beats one against the other before again trying to put one on top of the other while holding them up. At the end of the session, he takes the chip and places it on the cube, this time without any difficulty.

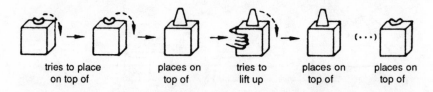

tries to place   places on   tries to   places on   places on
on top of   top of   lift up   top of   top of

Thus, after numerous attempts, A. at last succeeds at superposition. Right at the beginning of the session, he spotted the cube as a proper support object, and he returned to the cone as the object to be supported, as well as returning to the chip following his initial failure. Throughout the session, he tries a variety of possibilities of putting things together, taking their previously explored characteristics into account. The fortuitous arrival of the chip next to one end of the tube led him on. While his intentions were clear, he encountered difficulties in manipulating the objects and in choosing the right ones. A. did not manage to introduce the chip into the tube.

In the following example, a similar envelopment is attempted:

L. *at 12;4,* after manipulating various objects, looks carefully at the tube and then uses it to touch and shove the ball of cotton and then the ball of paper.

observes   touches   touch-shoves

In this effort at putting things in relation one to the other, the tube seems like a prolongation of the hand.

L. once more observes the tube and then successively introduces different fingers into the openings.

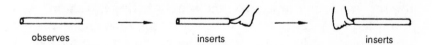

observes   inserts   inserts

L. has discovered the openings. Here, the envelopment concerns parts of her own body and only very gradually does she come to use other objects for the purpose.

L. (keeping her index finger in the opening of the tube) starts pushing other objects—the round bead, and then once more the ball of paper, which she examines and feels before pushing it with the tube while exerting more and more pressure on the tube.

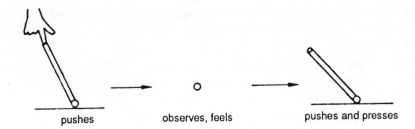

pushes   observes, feels   pushes and presses

Is this another kind of instrumental action, or should it be considered the beginnings of an attempt at covering the paper ball with the tube?

A little later, L. takes hold of a stick and brings it near the opening of the tube. Then she introduces her fingers into the opening several times.

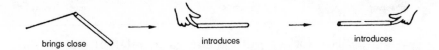

brings close   introduces   introduces

For the first time, L. brings two objects together held in either hand. It is no longer a matter of simply shoving something with the tube. Though it was very rapidly done, this was perhaps her first attempt at inserting one object into another and perhaps her subsequent finger action was prompted by a desire to make sure that the tube really was the kind of object into which something might be inserted. What follows lends support to this idea.

L. takes the bead and tries in vain to insert it into the tube (the bead is too large to fit). She puts the bead and then the tube in her mouth. Then she again inserts her finger into the tube.

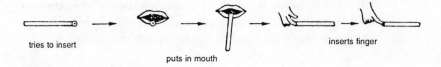

tries to insert   inserts finger

puts in mouth

L.'s intention is now obvious: She wishes to insert the bead into the tube. But rather than seek a more suitable object for insertion, she returns to using parts of her own body. A little later, she does try other objects.

L. takes a stick and tries to insert it into the tube, but she does not succeed because she does not properly align them. Next, after having examined the grid, she passes the stick through it several times. She then takes a ball of paper and perseveres in pushing it against the opening of the tube, but again the diameter is slightly too large. This puts an end to L.'s efforts, which have lasted nearly 10 minutes.

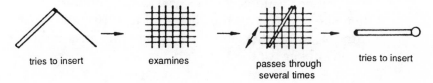

tries to insert   examines   passes through   tries to insert
                                       several times

L. made a correct choice in taking the stick in her search for something to insert into the tube, but her manipulative skills were not up to the task. With another "container" (i.e., the grid), she succeeded easily in inserting the stick and repeated the process several times, but when she returned to the tube, again she did not succeed. At the beginning of the session, she did not appear to have a definite plan, and the idea of enveloping one thing with another emerged only gradually after handling, exploring, and bringing together various objects. Merely adumbrated at first, the idea gradually became more definite, especially when she inserted her finger into the tube. The simultaneity of inserting her finger into one end of the tube and shoving the bead with the other is an important event on the road to discovering the possibility of enveloping one object with another. Just as for A., the actual envelopment proves difficult due to her level of manipulative skills and her choice of objects, which leads her back to using her own body, the importance of which was discussed in the preceding chapter.

At about 15 months of age, explorations last longer, and the children's intentions are clearer. More and more frequently, the choice of objects seems to be made in accordance with a plan, and the actions are better coordinated toward resolving the problems the children seem to be facing. The actual examination of the objects is more rapid and precise. Combinations of objects are more frequent and give rise to many variations. There follow two examples of *putting into,* a particularly frequent action in our observations of children about 15 months of age.

L. at 14;6 takes the small plastic stick and introduces it into one of the apertures of the grid. L. takes hold of a large rubber band and looks at it while holding it, then she places it on the stick as if to surround it. She withdraws the stick and then puts it back inside the round rubber band.

The action of *putting into* does not raise any practical problems and is facilitated by the choice of objects. L. used an object she happened to come across and varied her action in an apparent exploration of the container–content relationship, using the rubber band first in the one role and then in the other. These variations are pursued a little later with other objects:

L. takes a paper ball and places it in one of the apertures of the grid. She then takes a bead and places it in one of the adjoining apertures. She next tries several times to take the bead out of the grid, but it slips between her fingers. By contrast, she easily removes the ball of paper. After yet another effort to remove the bead, L. puts the ball of paper back into the grid, lifts the grid with both hands, and thus liberates both ball and bead. She casts a glance at the observer as if asking for her discovery and success to be witnessed. Next, she places the grid on the two objects, thus confining them within the apertures, and repeats the action a little later.

Faced with the difficulty of emptying the grid, L. discovers a new way to do so (i.e., lifting it up), and she goes on to give the grid an active role by covering the bead and the ball.

What is new in this example is the inversion of the active–passive roles of the objects in achieving the goal of envelopment. This concentration on ways of combining and separating objects is the theme in the following example also.

Ch. at 15;4 takes the conical bead and looks at it from all sides. Seeing a hole, he touches it with his index finger, then he puts down the bead. Next, he takes the tube, examines it attentively, touches one of its extremities, then stops, searches among the objects, and (touching the bead more or less by chance) is once again interested in it. Straightaway he establishes contact between the two things, placing one in prolongation of the other (which does he want to insert in the other?) He does not pursue this line of experimentation, lets go the bead, and takes up the small plastic stick, which he tries to insert into the tube, but does not persevere when he encounters some difficulty. (Ch. seems puzzled.) He looks questioningly at the observer. Letting go the plastic stick, he takes up the piece of spaghetti, which he looks at carefully. Then he once more examines the tube. Again he observes the spaghetti before deciding to insert it into the tube. He stretches his arms far apart in order to hold the two objects by their farther extremities, and he does not succeed in aligning them correctly.

A fairly brief exploration of the objects was all Ch. needed to distinguish possible container and content objects.

His choice was correct, and Ch. seemed disappointed at his lack of success. After some further exploration, Ch. returned to his initial pursuit:

Ch. sticks the spaghetti some way into the modeling clay and looks at the hole he has made. Letting go the spaghetti, he scratches the ball of clay with his finger, takes up the tube, and shoves it against the clay. (At this moment his attention is attracted to the free end of the tube.) He inserts his index finger into one end, then does so at the other end of the tube, then at the first end again, then inserts both index fingers, one at each end. Taking his fingers out of the tube, he quickly looks over the whole collection of things and again picks out the spaghetti. He then easily inserts it into the tube, holding both objects horizontally.

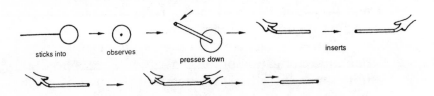

The repeated introduction of the fingers into the tube preceded the introduction of an object, which was chosen quite intentionally, and Ch. succeeded easily in overcoming the difficulties of alignment. But Ch. did not stop there:

Ch. inserts the spaghetti horizontally in the tube (the two objects are joined). Ch. then moves the tube to the vertical and watches the spaghetti slide out. He inserts it again, this time holding the tube in an oblique position (the spaghetti slides out of its own accord). Ch. inserts it again, but from the lower end of the tube held in the same position as before. He then turns the tube back to the horizontal (the construction holds). He then inclines the tube in the other direction and watches the spaghetti fall out. Ch.

reinserts the spaghetti into the lower end of the tube, still held obliquely, and then straightens the tube before the spaghetti can fall out. Ch. takes it out at the other end and then briefly puts the tube in his mouth. Holding the tube again in the oblique position, he inserts the spaghetti, which slips out. He starts again holding the spaghetti near the opening of the tube. He inserts it a little bit, pushes some more, then pushes on the free end of the spaghetti, and stops to observe the two objects, which now hold together, one prolonging the line of the other. He then takes the spaghetti out of the tube, puts the objects down, and stops experimenting.

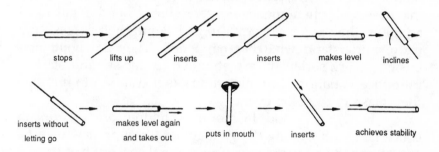

As soon as Ch. succeeded in inserting the spaghetti into the tube he undertook a series of what may properly be called "experiments," to discover the positions in which the two objects separate and those in which they stay put.

To sum up, the whole sequence comprises three phases:

1. A very brief exploration leading to consideration of possibilities of insertion

2. A longer phase in which suitable objects are sought; the choice is good, but success takes some time to achieve

3. A yet longer phase in which the effect of changes in approach and position are investigated.

On the basis of these examples, which are typical for all the children observed, it seems that between the ages of 12 and 15 months, children organize their explorations with greater precision, and they more rapidly come to concentrate on certain characteristics of the objects. Furthermore, the possibilities of combining objects (contiguity and envelopment), which are vaguely perceived around 12 months, after much fumbling, are more and more rapidly seen and tend to direct the initial explorations. Success in the construction of such combinations, which is often problematic because of the fine manipulative adjustments needed, begins to be achieved at about 15 months.

What is quite new are the experiments the children undertake once the desired combination is achieved. At 15 months, the children repeat their actions as if to make sure that the observed phenomena are reproducible and regular. In addition, they appear to want to go beyond their success and try to understand what has happened. They go about their business very seriously, are attentive to details, and start to introduce variations in their actions as if wanting to improve their mastery over the events.

Between 12 and 18 months, children are very much concerned with putting things together (creating new objects) and taking them apart again. This general concern has already been encountered in fragmenting activities, when the child started off with one object (e.g., a ball of cotton), which was pulled into many pieces, only to be reconstituted by putting the pieces together again. Though fragmenting may not present the same manipulative difficulties as inserting, both activities exert an equal fascination.

Behaviors observed between 18 and 24 months are the direct continuation of the aforementioned, but sequences become longer, and the observer increasingly gets the impression that the children, from the outset, start with a plan that coherently guides their actions. All the activities observed can be described either as *experimental* activities, of which an example has already been given and which now develop considerably, or as *frabricatory* activities, which develop little by little.

The experimentation and fabrication sequences fall into several categories. With the material we placed at the children's disposal, the following can be distinguished:

1. Threading

2. Piercing

3. Construction and parcel making (less frequent than the first two)

Between 12 and 18 months, the sequences comprised a long exploratory phase leading up to certain combinations of objects. However, in the following period, between 18 and 24 months, the combinations are reached increasingly rapidly, whereupon (depending on the activity) the children continue with experimentation or fabrication, the latter appearing quite clearly around 24 months.

Threading (Insertion into Apertures)

The most frequent way in which the children combine objects is by finding an object with openings and inserting another object that fits into it. These action sequences, as they are performed at 18 months, are generally made up as follows:

1. *An exploratory phase*, which is shorter than with the younger children but which also includes observation, choice of objects, and execution

2. *An experimental phase*, which becomes longer and more complex with age. Its different episodes develop coherently in accord with the questions the children appear to be asking themselves about the phenomena they are studying; unforeseen events may occur and may be exploited for the children's purposes. Though experimentation may vary with the individual child, main preoccupations and the way in which the children proceed are the same for all.

E. at 18;7 observes the piece of spaghetti and then the conic
  bead, the apertures of which he explores with his
  index finger. He then takes the tube and brings it
  close to the bead as if he wanted to insert the latter.
  After having put the bead into his mouth, he once
  again brings it close to the tube. Next he takes the
  spaghetti and without any difficulty inserts it into the
  bead. E. shoves the spaghetti all the way through the
  bead and then holds the spaghetti still and glides the
  bead along it. He starts again, now holding the bead
  still and shoving the spaghetti through it.

  E. seems to concentrate on varying the movement of the
two objects and experiments with holding one of them still
(passive) and moving the other one (active), and vice versa.

With the bead on the spaghetti, E. holds the latter at both
  ends and inclines it one way and then the other. He
  lets go the upper end and fixedly observes the movement of the bead. Wanting to start again from the
  horizontal position, he makes too sharp a movement
  and the spaghetti breaks.

  In E.'s new variation, he gets one of the objects (the
bead) to move by acting on another object. He seems to
anticipate the possible separation of the two objects and to
prevent it by always keeping hold of the lower end of the
spaghetti. The breakage diverts his attention.

E. lets the bead fall from the piece of spaghetti that stayed in
  his hand. He picks up the other bit of spaghetti and
  threads it into the bead on the floor. Picking up the
  bead, he introduces the remainder of the spaghetti
  into the other end of the bead. He ejects the bit he
  first introduced.

  Was his intention to continue his original activity by
reconstituting the spaghetti (by simply aligning the pieces
inside the bead)?

Keeping the larger piece of spaghetti in the bead, he pushes
the bead to the middle of it, then takes the smaller
piece and brings it near one end of the larger piece
and then near the other end. He repeats these actions
with the small plastic stick.

It certainly seems that the broken spaghetti raises
problems for E. Is he still trying to put the pieces together again
(now by aligning them outside the bead and also by making an
attempt with a similar object)?

Pulling hard on the piece of spaghetti threaded through the
bead, pulling first from one side, then from the other,
E. breaks it once more. (Did he do so intentionally?
Perhaps). He repeats the action several times and
breaks the remainder of the spaghetti into small
pieces. He threads the last piece through the
bead on the floor, and then adds two other pieces.
Picking up the bead in one hand and turning it
around rapidly, he attempts to thread in another
piece. Then he slowly inclines the bead and empties it
of its contents.

Faced with the impossibility of reconstituting the original whole, E. actively tries doing the breaking, which had
previously proved so irksome. He several times reproduces the
break just as it happened the first time. He then integrates
parts of the broken object within the previous action (which
had encompassed the whole). But threading the pieces of
spaghetti then becomes more like assembling pieces in a
container (for the bead is on the floor), which leads E. to
preoccupations that are more like those described in the
preceding chapter.

This example thus comprises three phases:

1. The first is quite brief. While exploring some
   objects, E. discovers the possibility of threading
   something through the bead, and after a false start,
   E. discovers an object suitable for the purpose.

2. In the second, which is considerably longer, E. is intrigued by his mobile and studies it by repeating the setup. He systematically varies the ways in which he can move the two objects, one in relation to the other. At first, centered on his own action, he shoves each of the objects in turn, imparting to them an active and then a passive role. Subsequently, he brings about the movement of one of the objects by changing the position of the other. This is close to *detour behavior* (the means used are not immediately directed toward the end in view). Here, E. lets an exterior force—gravity—do the work, instead of directly acting on the objects himself.

3. In the third, which grew out of an unforeseen event, E. tries in various ways to continue his investigations, whereupon, after reproducing the disturbing event several times, he changes his activity. While continuing within the range of threading activities, he abandons his observation of kinetics in favor of grouping the pieces.

This example illustrates the children's interest around 18 months in the kinetics they observe when they thread one object onto another. Their curiosity leads them to wonder about the phenomenon, which they bring about repeatedly in order to see closely what happens, and they vary the conditions as if wanting to relate cause and effect.

The same interest is found some months later in children aged about 24 months. At this age, the sequences become longer still, and the problems the children concern themselves with appear even more clearly. Threading becomes immediate for all the children, and the experimental phases of the sequences become more elaborate. Proceeding by stages, the children come nearer to defining and controlling the role of each object in relation to the other, the part played by their own action, and so on.

Immediate threading is followed by a lengthy experimental phase. E. (at 24;13) is tireless in varying his actions, which are thoroughly detailed, and he is very much taken up with the discovery and mastery of various aspects of threading. He first observes different stages of threading by precisely repeating his actions and later concentrates on particular movements.

E. introduces the spaghetti into the rubber band and then into the grid (both lying on the floor). He then inserts the spaghetti into the tube held vertically. Next, he inclines the tube a little (the tube is held too close to the floor for the spaghetti to slide out). He repeats the action with the tube several times.

For a better understanding of the fall of the spaghetti, E. repeats the action with variations; he seeks to control the movement of the spaghetti by making it fall out and especially by trying various ways of preventing it from falling out.

E. introduces the spaghetti into the lower end of the tube and then tilts the tube back to horizontal. He pushes the spaghetti some more, paying great attention to its emergence at the far end. Continuing, he slightly tilts the tube (the spaghetti starts to slide). Before it slides out entirely, he pushes it back inside the tube. Because the tube is still tilted, the spaghetti starts sliding again as soon as he takes his hand away. He rectifies it by bringing the tube back to the horizontal (the spaghetti stops sliding). He takes the spaghetti out and reintroduces it, the tube being slightly inclined. With one hand, he pushes the spaghetti through the tube, and with the other, he stops up the far opening of the tube (the spaghetti cannot emerge). He withdraws the spaghetti and introduces it again. He repeats the action several times, holding the tube horizontally.

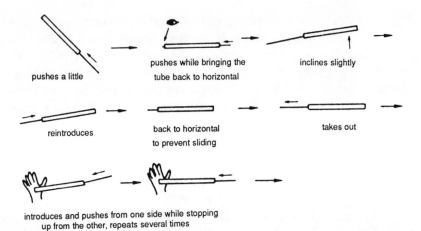

pushes a little

pushes while bringing the
tube back to horizontal

inclines slightly

reintroduces

back to horizontal
to prevent sliding

takes out

introduces and pushes from one side while stopping
up from the other, repeats several times

In this way, E. observes that by inclining the tube, he can make the spaghetti fall out, that by pushing it back into the tube he can stop it for a moment, and that by holding the tube horizontally or by blocking the exit he can prevent the spaghetti from falling out. All variations are carried out very deliberately as if in slow motion, which makes for better observation on E.'s part. Next, he concentrates on various ways of allowing the spaghetti to escape.

E. once more introduces the spaghetti (in the inclined position) from the top without blocking the exit. He watches the spaghetti emerge and then makes the end disappear again by pulling back a little. He repeats the action, but this time he lets the spaghetti drop out. He starts again with the tube held vertically some distance from the floor. Continuing in the horizontal position, he discovers a new technique, impelling the spaghetti strongly so that it traverses the tube entirely and flies out at the far end.

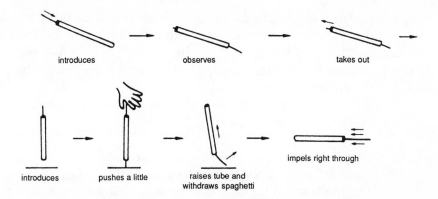

introduces   observes   takes out

introduces   pushes a little   raises tube and
withdraws spaghetti   impels right through

He repeats these various actions several times, using the three different positions of the tube, and he then combines the three positions in one operation:

E. introduces the spaghetti into the tube held horizontally. He then tilts the tube slowly and watches the spaghetti emerge. He continues the movement until the tube is vertical. He then raises the tube so that the spaghetti (until then supported by the floor) can fall out.

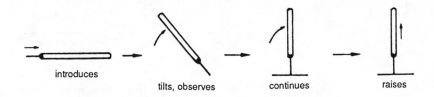

introduces   tilts, observes   continues   raises

During quite a long time, he repeats the experiments numerous times with great care and seriousness of purpose.

This example shows a series of experiments carried out systematically. The problems are raised clearly one after the other and examined coherently. E. studies how the spaghetti can be prevented from falling out: by pushing it back (temporary effect), by holding everything in the horizontal position, and by blocking the exit. Next, he studies various ways of separating the two objects: (a) in the inclined position, either by letting the spaghetti slide or by withdrawing it; (b) in the vertical position, by letting the spaghetti slide or by raising the tube; (c) in the horizontal position, by impelling the spaghetti with sufficient force.

The following example with the same two objects shows a different approach:

B. *at 23;18* pretends to eat using the tube and then the spaghetti as a spoon. Then he inserts the spaghetti into the tube in the vertical position. No sooner does he see the tip of the spaghetti emerge than he withdraws it. He reinserts the spaghetti and this time lets it go (the spaghetti is stopped by the floor). B. raises the tube in a series of small movements and gradually uncovers the spaghetti. Then he puts the tube right down again.

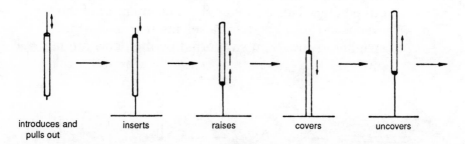

introduces and   inserts   raises   covers   uncovers
pulls out

B.'s interest in the appearance and disappearance of the object is immediate, and it may be asked whether he uses the tube also to *mark* the spaghetti—to divide the continuous aspect of this object (without breaking it). Several variations follow:

B. again hides the spaghetti, but it slides out on the floor. He picks it up again and partially covers it with the tube in the horizontal position. He continues to shove the spaghetti slowly while accompanying his gesture by saying "pa . . . pa . . . pa . . ." and looking fixedly at the free end of the tube. As soon as he sees the spaghetti appear, he pulls a little on the emerging end, again saying "pa . . . pa . . . pa . . . ," and then shoves the spaghetti back into the tube until it comes up against his hand holding the other end.

In the aforementioned series, B. tries with rhythmical movements to master the effects of his action. He seems to want to measure from what point on the spaghetti appears or disappears. In the following sequence, when he changes the position and the role of the two objects, he pursues a different purpose (i.e., he tries to keep the two objects together).

Having withdrawn the spaghetti, B. reintroduces it into the tube held obliquely. He tilts the tube back to the horizontal while watching the exit end. With the spaghetti jutting out an equal amount at both ends of the tube, B. stands up holding his assemblage, but the spaghetti escapes as he straightens up. He starts again, this time introducing the spaghetti into the lower end of the tube with small regular movements while he watches the exit. Again he stands up, and again the spaghetti escapes.

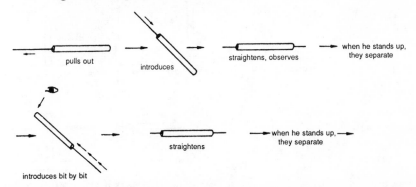

After failing to maintain the two objects in a stable position (perhaps he assembled them to make a new unit), he takes up again, with variations, his previous activity of making the spaghetti appear and disappear.

B. introduces the spaghetti into the tube, raises the tube a
    little, observes, and then lets go. He next observes the
    spaghetti, which he raises a little out of the tube. He
    takes hold of the tube at the lower end close to the
    floor and raps gently on the floor with it, thus making
    the spaghetti appear and disappear in rapid suc-
    cession. Then he turns the tube back to the horizon-
    tal, saying "pan." The spaghetti now protrudes a little
    at one end. Quickly, he reverses the direction of the
    tube. The spaghetti slides back into the tube and
    protrudes a little at the other end. He puts the tube
    containing the spaghetti back on the floor in a vertical
    position, saying "pa . . . pa . . . pa . . . ." He then
    raises the tube, uncovering the lower end of the spa-
    ghetti. Once more he covers it, saying "pa . . . pa . . .
    pa . . ." and then uncovers it all the way—the two
    objects come apart. "Encore!" he says, and, holding
    up the spaghetti obliquely, he partially covers it with
    the tube and continues to push the spaghetti upward
    into the tube, saying "pa." With a change of hand, he
    returns everything to the floor and says "pa!" when
    the spaghetti is covered once more.

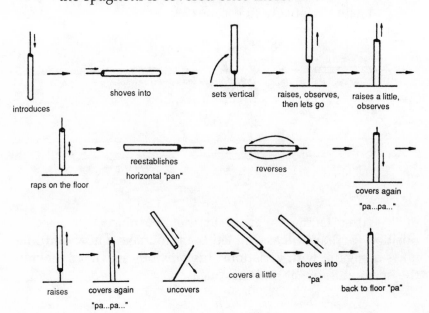

The example shows several variations during the search for mastery of the possibilities for hiding the spaghetti and making it appear again. B. goes about his business with great seriousness and is visibly pleased whenever he makes some advance. The sequence also shows inferences being made from the result of one action, thus raising new problems, which entail new activities with anticipation of the possible results, and so forth.

All the examples of threading by children ages 18 to 24 months illustrate the development of behaviors that may properly be called "experimental." In their quest for mastery, the children vary either the position of the objects or the objects themselves within the same experimental procedure.

Though there are considerable similarities among all our observations at the same age, there are differences in the problems on which the infants focus their attention. Such differences occur across different children, but differences also arise within the same action sequence pursued by one child. For instance, the children may focus on separating two objects they have combined and observe the various possible motions brought about by gravity or by their own action (e.g., they may catch a falling object or observe it as it falls free). They may also treat the combination of two objects quite differently, with attention focused on the possibilities of making one of the objects disappear within the other. B., with his careful repeated gestures—lengthening or shortening the visible portion by small, nearly equal amounts—may suggest measuring activities that are pursued by much older children. A rather similar activity with "dividing" a piece of string was described earlier.

In their experimentation based on threading actions, the children are interested mainly in the kinetics of the situation. However, as is shown in the following description, activities based on piercing tend toward another line of exploration—namely, the fabrication of new objects. But before discussing these fabrication activities, it should be stressed that such experimentation is only possible due to a parallel development of logical capacity, which enables the children in this age group (a) to choose adequate and equivalent objects, (b) to seriate their actions in a temporal order adapted to the aim pursued, and (c) to draw inferences from the effects observed. From this point of view, the final phase of a long experimental sequence performed by a child of 25 months is worth describing:

> K. *at* 25;9 (after having studied the movements of the spaghetti, the small stick, the bead, and the tube in various threading combinations) takes hold of the tube and the small stick. She places the tube on the floor and introduces the stick without letting it go (she wedges her finger into the opening of the tube to prevent the stick from slipping down). She then raises the whole and places it on the conical bead, which she maintains on the floor. She makes sure that the openings are well aligned. She then withdraws her finger, thus letting the stick fall, and lifts up the tube—the stick stands inserted into the bead!

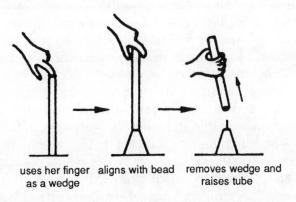

uses her finger   aligns with bead   removes wedge and
as a wedge   raises tube

For this elaborate action to succeed, detailed preparatory activities were necessary, which in turn depended on precise inferences and predictions. The temporal organization is especially critical: The effect aimed at cannot be achieved if the finger is withdrawn before the openings are aligned. The inference regarding the movement of the stick is also important: she knows that the stick will slide inside the tube and foresees that the stick will necessarily slide into the bead if the openings correspond.

Piercing

Piercing activities are another way of putting one thing into another, but now the object into which the other one is to be introduced does not have a preexisting opening. An object made of material suitable for the creation of an opening has to be chosen.

Among children below the age of 18 months, we observed only fleeting and isolated instances of scratching an object or shoving at it (with a finger or with another object). At about 18 months, piercing occurs sporadically, but it becomes more frequent and better organized in longer and longer sequences until, at the age of about 24 months, activities based on piercing are just as prominent as those based on threading, and they frequently alternate with threading.

Similar to what happens in threading, the long objects are used for piercing. They include rigid ones (the two sticks), a flexible one (the pipe cleaner), and a brittle one (the spaghetti). Depending on the resistance of the objects, the sequences occur differently.

Here is an example of a sequence with a flexible object:

E. *at 18;4* attentively observes the ball of modeling clay and the pipe cleaner in turn. Then he lightly pricks the clay with the pipe cleaner, again observes the latter, and returns to the clay. Now he presses the pipe cleaner into the clay a little harder, and it bends.

E. presumably assimilated the properties of the pipe cleaner to those of a stick, and he did not expect it to bend. Intrigued by this effect, he set about experimenting by using different objects and by graduating his action:

E. next presses the pipe cleaner onto a polystyrene chip, then he returns to the clay, bending the cleaner once again. He once more sticks it into the polystyrene after scratching the clay a little with the cleaner. Then he presses the cleaner boldly into the clay, whereupon the pipe cleaner is bent in two. E. pushes some more, and the pipe cleaner forms a complicated zig-zag. E. takes up the polystyrene chip and, despite difficulties of alignment, manages to prick it with the pipe cleaner. He sets out to repeat the action, but when he lifts the pipe cleaner, the polystyrene chip comes up with it. He rapidly shakes the combined objects in order to separate them, and then he uses the pipe cleaner to pierce the ball of clay and the chip alternately.

While bringing about the transformation of one object (the pipe cleaner), E. assiduously investigates the resistance of the other two objects.

The example illustrates how piercing becomes part of a detailed examination of the properties of objects. One unforeseen event—the bending of the pipe cleaner—is investigated further, but another—the bonding of the pipe cleaner and the polystyrene chip—is not. Interest in the joining of the two objects is seen in children a few months older, when it takes on fresh meaning as a way of creating new objects.

Piercing activities are thus constructed little by little at the age of about 18 months. This is the age when the infants not only use objects with apertures for their favorite activity of putting into, but also discover the possibility of using objects without apertures. Among these objects, children choose objects that are not hard. While threading appears earlier, there is now a rather different focus of interest. The infants are drawn not so much to the *kinetics of the situation* as to the *static result of assemblage*. The making of new objects by piercings, done deliberately and immediately appears more clearly at the age of about 24 months. What is being made is not always decided in advance. Generally, it is the fact of two objects holding together that rivets the infant's attention. At this moment, the children tend to interrupt their piercings in order to consider the new object. Subsequently, fabrication is taken up for its own sake, and the children go about reproducing the object with the same or similar materials. They may also add elements, thus creating more and more sophisticated objects that are contemplated, shown, and sometimes named.

These fabrications are usually achieved by using the sticks or the spaghetti, in order to pierce the cotton ball, the polystyrene chip, or the modeling clay. The following is an example of an infant who pursued this activity during three consecutive sessions:

K. at 22;20 (after trying various ways of threading the spaghetti through the tube) starts sticking the spaghetti into the ball of modeling clay. She withdraws it, pulling off a small piece of clay. She attentively observes the end of the spaghetti to which a fragment of clay remains attached. She blows on it as if it were a match. Repeatedly, in the same way, she detaches a piece of clay, observes the "match," blows on it forcibly, and presents it to the observer while vocalizing.

Initially, it seemed that K. wanted to fragment the clay, using the spaghetti as an instrument. However, on noticing that the clay adhered to the spaghetti, she immediately gave it a symbolic meaning and pretended it was a match. Observed a month later, K. immediately takes up the same activity and fabricates a "match." She continues by making a different object:

K. at 24;4, taking hold of the ball of clay and the small stick, detaches a piece of clay with the stick and blows on the end of the stick. She repeats the operation several times. Because she always introduces the stick at the same place, she eventually implants the stick firmly into the ball of clay. She lifts up the stick with the ball attached, but she pays no attention to this new assemblage. Not until a little later, after having observed the hole in the clay produced by the stick, does she reunite the two and observe the ensemble attentively. She takes it apart and reconstructs it several times.

The new fabrication involving the whole ball resembles the first (the match), but it is nevertheless distinct: K. does not blow on it. The new object also is fabricated several times, but no explicit meaning is imparted to it. K. is interested both in the assemblage, which she observes, and in the deep hole, which she observes after she separates the two elements. A month later, she uses this double observation to make something else:

K. at 25;9 pushes the spaghetti through a bead and then forces the stick into the ball of modeling clay. By pushing hard and turning the stick, she succeeds in piercing the ball right through. She takes the stick out and puts it in again several times. The hole is now larger, and she pushes the stick in as if the ball of clay were a bead.

Therefore, with the stick and the ball of clay, she did something similar to what she had done with the spaghetti and the bead at the beginning of the session. Now she returns to the fabrication started at 24;4:

K. again puts the stick into the clay but not into the hole she made. When the stick is well in, she lifts it up—the two objects hold together. She beats on the floor with this "hammer."

By using the assemblage to beat with, K. does seem to pretend that the new object is a hammer, but it is less well defined than other new objects, for it is neither contemplated, nor shown, nor taken apart, nor duplicated.

Leaving the stick planted in the clay, she takes hold of the spaghetti and shoves it into the clay near the stick. The spaghetti breaks, but one piece remains stuck in the clay. "Broke!" she says. Then she shows the whole to the observer and exclaims "Two!" After having contemplated her creation for a long time, K. sets it down in front of her. She then breaks the remaining spaghetti and plants one of the pieces in the clay, crying "Two!" and proudly shows off the result. She breaks off other bits of spaghetti and adds them to the ball of clay. For the last piece, she shouts "Two!" even before planting it. She then presents her fabrication with a joyous "The two!" while looking around among the materials. She withdraws the stick she had planted in the beginning, leaving only the bits of spaghetti. Then she places her creation on a piece of paper.

The unforeseen breakage of the spaghetti is not taken up for its own sake, but it becomes integrated into K.'s creation. Her interest in making a new object is enriched by the concern with making a logical collection of identical units (the bits of spaghetti are of approximately the same length, and the stick is eliminated).

From about 24 months on (unlike younger children), the children start to make new objects by following a plan of action apparently conceived at the outset. The new productions are frequently named. C., for example, produced an object almost identical to K.'s final clay–spaghetti assemblage and called it "bébête" (i.e., little animal).

Construction and Parcel Making

In addition to the activities described, other ways of combining objects were observed, notably putting one thing on top of another. These combinations reflect both an interest in making something new and an interest in putting things together and taking them apart. The children, for example, build towers and then destroy them, which tends to lead to experimentation. With the materials we put at their disposal, these activities were, however, much less frequent than threading and piercing.

Tower Building

An early example of putting one thing on another was already described. Between the ages of 18 and 24 months, some more elaborate constructions were observed and the builders' interest in equilibrium and its destruction was very well sustained. Because the children had few objects at their disposal suitable for this kind of activity (two blocks and a bead), they could not go very far with their experiments. Nevertheless, we would like to give an example because of an essential difference from the previously described assemblages: Tower building depends on contiguity and static equilibrium, not on insertion.

> *N. at 19 months* takes hold of a cube and a rectangular block and places them end to end. He next places the rectangular block vertically on the floor and then places the cube on top. He then takes a stick and shoves the cube, so the tower collapses.

N. thus immediately starts building a tower after having placed his two blocks in line. Right from the start, he also shows the dual interest in balancing (static assemblage) and letting slide (separation and movement). N. starts again and introduces a third component:

> *N.* takes the rectangular block and then the conical bead, and places them end to end. Taking hold of the cube, he places the rectangular block vertically on the floor, puts the cube on top, hesitates to take the tube, then finally takes the conical bead and places it on top of the cube. He stops for a moment to observe his handiwork. Then he looks for and finds the tube, with which he shoves at the base of the tower, so it collapses.

Again, N. starts in a similar way: Before actually building the tower, he puts his new component end-to-end with one of the other ones. The tower, once built, is again destroyed with a similar instrument, the tube replacing the stick. The fact that he stops to look at his work indicates his interest in creating something new. Also of note is a difference in how he destroys the tower: The first time, he pushed the upper component; this time, he pushed at the bottom. (Was this variation intentional?)

The three components having remained next to one another on the floor, N. first tries to erect them as they are, as if they still held together. He then picks them up one after the other, and reconstitutes his tower. Taking the stick, he pushes the middle component. The base remains vertical, and with a second shove, he upsets it too.

Because he again changed the point of application for knocking down the tower, it does seem as if he were experimenting.

Parcel Making

From 18 months on, another way of combining objects is observed: parcel making (i.e., the children use the sheet of paper or the piece of cloth to wrap other objects). Here, as in the threading activities, there is an interest in making things disappear and appear again, but parcel making is more like tower building, in that there is not the same sort of penetration of objects that there is in threading or piercing. However, in parcel making, there is no interest in the kinetic separation of the objects.

N. *at 19 months* attentively observes the cloth, feeling it, crushing it, and spreading it out. Next, holding it with one hand, he places the ball of modeling clay on it. He turns both objects over into his other hand and observes for a moment what has happened: The ball of clay has disappeared under the cloth. He pulls the cloth a little bit to the side as if to make sure that the ball is still there. Then he lifts off the cloth entirely.

Intrigued by the disappearance of the ball of clay, N. repeats, as follows:

> Several times, with great attention, N. covers the ball of clay on the floor with the cloth. Then he picks it up through the cloth and turns the whole over in his hand, making the ball visible. Finally he tries to wrap the ball of clay by raising the edges of the cloth.

N. systematically brings about the disappearance and reappearance of the ball of clay by experimenting with the relationships above and beneath.

Two months later, N. returns to the problem:

> N. at 21;3 takes the ball of clay and, immediately afterward, the cloth. He puts the ball in the cloth and wraps it up completely.

N. thus succeeds in hiding the ball in a new way (i.e., by no longer by simply having it beneath the cloth but by using the cloth as a wrapper). He experiments with the technique by first of all substituting the sheet of paper for the cloth:

> The ball of modeling clay having rolled toward the piece of paper, N. immediately seizes the latter in order to wrap up the ball: He crimps the paper minutely against the ball.

Subsequently, N. twice changes the content:

> Having taken hold of the ball of cotton, N. puts the empty piece of paper on the floor. He then notices the bulge left by the ball of clay in the paper. He immediately turns the paper over and deposits the cotton ball into the hollow, whereupon he wraps the parcel, pressing hard on the paper so that the parcel will hold. Next, he withdraws the cotton ball, observing carefully the new hollow left in the paper, and he then puts in two

beads, after having first placed them in the hollow of the board (which is slightly curved longitudinally) and then in the grid.

For a while, N. seems less interested in the appearance and disappearance of the content objects than in the particularities of the container. That is, the piece of paper, unlike the cloth, conserves an imprint of the objects that were wrapped in it; the paper is more of a receptacle, like the board with its hollow, or the grid with its apertures. N. returns to the possibility of totally enclosing something in this pliable container:

N. wraps the beads, crushing the paper for a long while. He then delicately opens the parcel a little way and is delighted when he sees the beads. He wraps them up again carefully until he has a package that will really hold, which he then deposits between his legs.

The interest in hiding one thing in another is in the foreground here again. Experimenting with the permanence of objects leads N. to make a new object, which differs from other creations, in that his parcel contains a hidden object.

A month later, N.'s curiosity is still not satisfied, and he continues:

N. at 22;7 immediately starts wrapping the ball of modeling clay in the sheet of paper, then places the parcel between his legs and looks at it. He repeats the operation several times, observes the parcel, and shows it to another child while vocalizing. Next, N. substitutes the cloth for the paper. Once he has wrapped up the modeling clay, he opens the cloth a little bit, shows the clay to the observer and explains "A é caché!" [It is hidden], then he closes the parcel and places it on the floor. He remakes the parcel, several times commenting "Caché! Caché!" but then he makes a false move, and the ball slides out on the floor. N. covers it by placing the cloth over it, and then folds the cloth as if the ball of clay were above it and not beneath it. He lifts it up and realizes that the ball of clay is still on the floor. He picks up the ball and several times wraps it up correctly. He continues, using the paper instead of the cloth and the cotton ball instead of the clay. Then he uses the beads instead of the cotton ball, ever repeating "Caché!" At one time, he holds out his parcel to another child as if it were a present.

N. thus commented on his trials and made an object that was apparently a symbolic present. The surprising element in this example is that N. raises the problem of the permanent object in a series of experiments (analogous to situations proposed by Piaget, 1937, pp. 55–64) in which N. simultaneously plays the parts of the researcher and the subject.

Summary and Conclusions

In the research described in this chapter, we presented the infants with a collection of varied objects, most of which were unique in the collection; some of the objects could be fragmented (cotton wool, modeling clay, etc.), others had holes (beads, tube, etc.), and yet others could be made to change their shape without being readily fragmentable (string, rubber band, etc.)

With these materials, the youngest infants pursued the same activities as those described in Chapter 1, especially in the beginning of each session. But very soon (from the age of 12–13 months), the materials gave rise to other activities, which changed further with increasing age. However, a common feature of most of these activities was the interest they revealed in the relations between parts and the whole, whether an object is broken into pieces or several objects are combined to form a new entity.

With the materials in the first research study (rods, balls of modeling clay, nesting cubes), the main action from 12 months on consisted in putting one object into another, an action that may mean uniting two objects to form a single object. With the materials of this second research study, the main action between the ages of approximately 12 and 16 months consists in fragmenting an object (an action that started from a single object and then created several or many parts). One of the objects presented to the children was very easy to fragment (i.e., the ball of cotton). With this object, sustained interest was observed in tearing it into smaller and smaller pieces. This is done very systematically by way of two different procedures. Infants younger than our subjects commonly enjoy crumbling a biscuit or pulling a piece of bread to bits, but it is rare in everyday life that they are allowed to follow all the way through. Further, from another point of view, neither a biscuit nor a piece of bread lends itself readily to being stuck together again.

Just as *putting into* is frequently followed by *taking out*, so taking to bits is frequently followed by putting together again.

The materials placed at the infants' disposal did not include anything that readily could be used as a container, so the combining of objects (e.g., by putting one into the other) developed progressively in spontaneously structured sequences. Combining took the form of threading, piercing, building, and making parcels. Activities based on threading were observed earlier than the others, which, in the main, were observed between 18 and 24 months. These activities were contemporaneous with other activities dealing with only one object—that is, shape changing (the piece of string and the rubber band).

It seems that putting-into activities are at the origin of the threading and piercing activities, while putting-on-top-of and putting-up-against activities lead to tower building. Making parcels, an activity that makes its appearance somewhat later, combines putting-into with putting-on-top-of.

Once they succeed in combining several objects in these

ways, the infants concern themselves with an increasingly large range of problems, thanks to the variety of objects at their disposal. The children's interest comes to be centered on either:

- Creating stable relationships between objects (e.g., by inserting one object into another), leading to the creation of new objects, the components of which hold together by insertion or superposition,

- Or creating unstable relationships (e.g., by threading two objects together), which leads to studying mainly the movements of the objects as regards direction of movement and orientation of the immobile object, as well as causality.

Activities in these two fields of interest (which are complementary and may be combined in the pursuits of older children) raise new problems and call for aims and methods that differ from those observed among the younger children. The distinction was made between experimentation and fabrication as modes of action, which differ also as regards other aspects of behavior. In fabrication, the children make clearly marked pauses, show their creation to another person, sometimes give it a name or symbolic meaning, and then go on to do something else. However, in experimentation, actions are linked and divided into stages without the achievement of an aim being so clearly marked.

The children ask themselves questions to which they try to find the answers systematically. Actions are repeated in the same way or by introducing variants in order to test the regularity of the observed phenomena. Answers entail new problems, which the children immediately set about resolving, and so on.

Experimentation is linked most closely to threading activities and mainly concerns the study of movement. The children show great interest in the gradual insertion of one object into another, and in the gradual disappearance of the inserted object until the two objects are practically one. And they are fascinated by the slow separation of the two objects until they are totally apart. (The children's interest in the problem of the parts and the whole has already been mentioned.)

Great interest in combining and then separating two objects is found earlier in the activity of fragmenting. Some of the children pay great attention to stretching the cotton ball slowly until a piece becomes detached. It seems that in one of the other transforming activities (i.e., changing the shape of a piece of string), a similar preoccupation can be discerned. In one of the examples, the infant seemed to be making divisions in this continuous object. This interpretation may seem hazardous, but it is given support by the description of a child making a piece of spaghetti appear and disappear in a tube, bit by bit while marking by voice each appearance and disappearance. This kind of marking of the parts of a continuous whole would seem to be the precursor of later measuring activities.

It is noteworthy that, among the older children, transforming activities are combined with those described. Fragmenting, in particular, may become part of fabrication and sometimes also of experimentation.

The prelogical activities highlighted in Chapter 1, of course, provide a foundation for the prephysical activities, which could not be carried out without a choice of suitable objects or a sequential ordering of actions.

Finally, the tenacity with which these very young children set about solving the problems they have discovered for themselves needs to be stressed. Their inflexibility of purpose and the seriousness and ingenuity with which they try to understand and use the objects placed at their disposal were truly remarkable.

CHAPTER 3

Infants and Symbolics

I. Lézine, H. Sinclair, M. Stambak, and
B. Inhelder
with the collaboration of
D. C. Dubon, D. Josse,
and M. Léonard

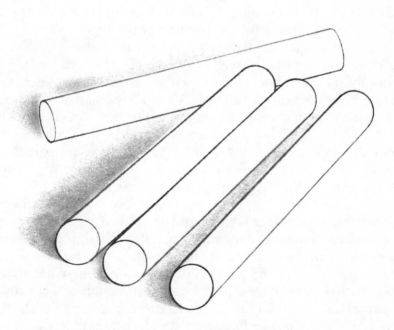

Introduction

In the preceding chapters, we were able to follow certain aspects of the transition from sensorimotor activity, with its *hic-et-nunc* (here-and-now) limitations, to conceptual thinking as observed in activities that become progressively better organized in space and time. Many of the behaviors observed can only be explained as stemming from reasoning based on representation—a representation either of the goal to be attained (e.g., the collections and the one-to-one correspondences of Chapter 1), or of an anticipated result of an experiment, based on previous experience, sometimes even with an organized sequence of variations (e.g., the children in Chapter 2 who foresaw the sliding out of a stick on one or the other side of a tube depending on the position of the tube).

Psychogenetic theory supposes the existence of certain forms of representation well before the age at which we started our observation. Recognition memory is both ontogenetically and phylogenetically primitive. Also, the mechanisms both for the assimilation of new objects into action schemes and for the reciprocal assimilation of schemes would be impossible without the infant's capacity to recognize certain properties of objects that render them suitable for integration into action schemes with the help of new accommodations.

The integration of a new object into an action scheme gives the object a meaning, and it is this meaning that is recognized (an object dangling from a string has, depending on the situation, the meaning of "to be swung," "to be looked at," or "to be listened to"). To verify by an action whether the object can indeed have one of these meanings always demands some kind of imitation. At the most primitive level, the grasping scheme is realized by a specific action that is adapted to certain properties of the object, in the sense that the hand or the mouth imitates the shape, size, and consistency of the object. However, it is only when these meanings can be represented by signifiers, which are no longer linked to each particular object and each particular action, that the child will be able to use such signifiers in his or her thinking in order to elaborate new constructions that go beyond the immediate present and the immediately visible space.

In the broad sense, every stage and substage that we can distinguish in the intelligent actions of children is accompanied by a certain type of representation that relies on "signifier(s) . . . constructed through imitation as the product of accommodation, that is continued as imitation and hence as images or interiorized imitations" (Piaget, 1946/1962, p. 273). In a narrower sense, representation is defined by Piaget as a differentiation between signifier and signified and as the capacity to evoke the meanings of events and objects in their absence. The construction and use of personal, interior symbols (such as mental images), or of symbols that can be shared (such as gestures or objects of play) or of conventional symbol systems (such as language) characterizes what is often called the "symbolic" or "semiotic function." This function plays a central role in the development of thought, and, in one of Piaget's dialectical spirals, it is simultaneously made possible by cognitive development and dependent on it.

During the first period of representational thinking, when children do not yet verbalize their thoughts, it is rare that an observer can actually capture the use of a symbol.

Piaget (1936/1952, Observation 180) reports observing the construction of a symbol-in-action by his daughter Lucienne at 1;4. Playing with her he hides a watch chain in a matchbox, leaving at first a slit wide enough for her to pull the chain out without opening the box further. Then he puts the chain into the box leaving only a tiny slit, sufficient for her to put her finger inside but not to pull the chain out. She attempts to pull the chain out but is baffled and stops trying; she looks closely at the slit and then opens and shuts her mouth several times. She then puts her finger into the box, opens it further and takes out the chain. Opening and shutting her mouth functions as a representation in action, as a "motor signifier or symbol" in Piaget's terms.

The nascent representation capacities function not only in the service of intelligence (for the solving of practical problems, for the organization of the living space, and for the exploration and knowledge of properties of objects and the ways they interact) but also in order to create situations that resemble real-life situations but are totally under the control of the subject: symbolic play. Symbolic or pretend play always implies imitation (of models seen in the past, absent in the present). In direct imitative behavior, the subject seems to try to accommodate as much as possible to the model whose image has been conserved, whereas in pretend play, reality is assimilated to the subject's activities and desires (allowing, for example, the young child to make building blocks into cars, her- or himself into a police officer, etc.)

Early "intuitive" thought that uses representations to solve practical problems develops into socialized scientific thought; early pretend play finds its continuation in imaginative creation.

In the study reported in this chapter, we tried to follow the development of pretend and symbolic play in children from about 1 to 3 years of age. The results have been reported extensively elsewhere (Inhelder et al., 1972). In this chapter, we only discuss the observations concerning the same age span studied in the research reported in Chapters 1 and 2 (i.e., from 10 to 27 months).

Experimental studies of *delayed imitation* (when a model is imitated well after its disappearance) and of pretending bring their own particular difficulties. If the observer was not present at the original scene, how can he or she expect to recognize the behavior of a child imitating this scene as imitative behavior? How, for example, does one interpret the behavior of a small girl waving her arms while looking at the upper corner of a window? This behavior will be clearly imitative only for an observer who previously saw the girl behaving in the same way, for example, in the presence of a butterfly beating its wings against a window pane. Many imitative behaviors go unnoticed because children are rarely observed continuously.

The observational method for this study was the same as that used in the other two. The objects given to the children in this study were very familiar to them: They were all objects that are used daily in the child-care centers, either in toy replicas or in actual size (e.g., cups, plates, spoons, a hairbrush, a broom, a sponge, as well as a doll, a teddy bear). It was thought that such well-known objects, which all the children had either used themselves or seen adults use, would lead to recognizable imitative and pretend behavior. In fact, this collection of objects constitutes a common experimental frame for both the children and the observers. Moreover, because the objects were well known to the children, they did not present any particular interest as novelties to become known, and the objects would therefore incite the children to engage in play behavior rather than in exploratory or experimental behavior. The results confirmed our expectations; whereas symbolic play behavior was rare in the two other studies, it occurred frequently with the objects presented in this study.

Materials

The children were seated on the floor with a collection of objects in front of them (placed randomly, but the identical disposition was repeated for every session). The objects were a baby bottle, a spoon, a plate, a mug, a toy potty-chair, a hand mirror, a hairbrush, a sponge, a toy broom, a toy feather duster, two dolls of different sizes, a teddy bear, a book, a small stick, some sheets of paper, and some pieces of cloth.

Population

All observations were made in Paris, in one day-care center, with 32 boys and 35 girls. Their developmental level was evaluated according to the Brunet–Lézine scale and was found to be normal. The children were also tested by the sensorimotor intelligence scale of Casati–Lézine (1968) once or several times during the period from 9 to 21 months.

Seven subjects were followed longitudinally once a month (with occasional absences). Taking account only of the age range discussed in this chapter, 145 sessions were recorded, with children observed either once, several times, or longitudinally (see Table 3.1).

Procedure

When the child was seated in front of the objects, one of the experimenters showed the objects to the child, one by one, naming each and adding that the child was free to play with all or any of them. The procedure was the same as in the other two studies, except that video equipment became available only during the last part of the research. Until then, two observers made minute-by-minute notes of all the activities, and they compared and adjusted their records immediately after the session.

Table 3.2 shows a sample extracted from one of the protocols (R. at 15 months):

As can be seen from the example, the columns indicate the object taken up first, the action carried out (with or without an object), the object acted upon, vocalizations, and looks. In the last column, the observer noted an interpretation whenever an action seemed interpretable. Such actions are of two different kinds: (1) well-executed conventional actions (e.g., brushing one's hair with the brush or sweeping the floor with the broom), or (2) pretend activities for which both observers concurred in their interpretation (e.g., "feeding the doll" when the child several times brings the spoon to the mouth of the doll).

Categorization of the Activities

These interpretable activities are to us the most interesting phenomena observed in this study. They have not been divided into two separate categories because, in many cases,

Table 3.1

Age in months	10/11	12	13	14	15	16	17	18	19	20	21
First observation number of children	6	10	8	5	4	4	4	1	2	4	4
Second observation number of children			2	3	2	3	3	4	1	1	2
Further observation number of children				2	3	4	5	7	7	5	4
Total number of observations	6	10	10	10	9	11	12	12	10	10	10

Age in months	22	23	24	25	26	27	28	29	30	31/32
First observation number of children	5	3	1		1	1				4
Second observation number of children	2			1	1					
Further observation number of children	5	5	6	2	2	2	1	2	3	8
Total number of observations	12	8	6	2	4	3	1	2	3	12

Table 3.2

Sample Extract from a Protocol

	Object 1	Action Object 2	Vocalization	Look	Interpretation
1st minute					
1	bottle	explores			
2	bottle	shakes			
3	bottle	discards			
4	spoon	puts on plate		looks at	feeding
		looks at			
		observer			
5				looks at	
6	spoon	scrapes plate		looks at	feeding
7		turns around			
		toward observer			
8		looks at observer			
9	hairbrush	feels with hand			

2nd minute

10	spoon	turns around and around	
11	spoon	puts on hairbrush	
13	spoon	pushes into hairbrush	"hè"
14			
15	spoon	presses on plate	
16	spoon	brings next to brush	
17	spoon	pushes	

3rd minute

18	hairbrush	takes and puts down	
19	doll	takes and turns around	"ah"
20			
21	doll	discards	
22	sponge	takes and throws	
23		crawls	
24		babbles	
25	scratches herself		

the distinction cannot be made. For example, when children put spoons into their mouths, are they simply performing a habitual action, or are they pretending to eat? With the older children, gestures, vocalizations, and sometimes utterances may make the distinction clear; with the younger children, it is often impossible to tell. In both kinds of actions, imitation is important. When the child sweeps the floor with the toy broom, she or he is imitating an adult; when the child puts the spoon into her or his mouth several times, the child is imitating her- or himself eating. At the same time, these activities are evidence of the child's knowledge of the object—they appear as action equivalents of the verbal definitions by usage (a spoon is for eating, soap is for washing, etc.) of 4- to 5-year-olds.

At the other extreme, a certain number of actions were noted that are not discussed here because they have no direct bearing on the development of imitation and pretend play. These are actions without an object (e.g., smiling, crying, crawling, and vocalizing or uttering words). The absence of a playmate (recall that the observer did not interact freely with the children) made the experimental situation totally unsuited to the study of communicative activities. The older subjects sometimes accompanied their pretend play with talk. Some of them even acted out elaborate scenes with the doll or the teddy bear, so the interpretation of their symbolic play was thus greatly facilitated and their utterances were used for the interpretation. Simple actions without objects diminish with age and almost disappear at about 15 months. A few of them are discussed in the later section regarding the children's knowledge of their own bodies.

The actions with objects that are not interpretable in the aforementioned sense can be divided into either actions with one object or actions with several objects. The former can be divided into those activities with one object where the object is brought into relation with the child's own body (e.g., licking the mirror) and those where the object is simply manipulated by itself. The proportion of activities with one object varies little with age. The proportion of activities with two or more objects increases between 10 and 18 months (from 8 to 22% of the total number of activities), and then it diminishes in favor of the interpretable activities, which increase from 0% to 10 months to 27% at 2 years.

Inventory of Behaviors in the Activities

Before attempting a sketch of the kind of development to be discerned in these various activities, we present an inventory of the behaviors observed in the four categories.

Activities with One Object Involving the Child's Own Body

- Oral activities: The children put into their mouths any of the small objects (brush, mirror, plate, broom etc.) and suck or bite it. When the object is an eating utensil, the activity may be classified as interpretable depending on the sequence in which it occurs and on the precision of the gestures. When children scrape the (empty) plate with a spoon, then lick the spoon, expressing glee, they obviously are pretending to eat. Similarly, when they bring the mug to their mouth with a precise gesture throwing their head back, they are pretending to drink.

- Touching, beating, or rubbing any part of the body with an object.

- Gently stroking or caressing any part of the body with an object.

- Putting an object onto a part of the body, such as on the knees (e.g., a mug—if the doll or the teddy bear is in the child's lap, it may of course be an interpretable activity, depending on the context), on the legs (e.g., putting the broom across both legs), on the belly (when done with the doll or the teddy bear, it may be an interpretable activity), or against part of the face (e.g., holding the mug against the forehead).

- Vestimentary activities: pulling, plucking, folding, and so forth, the clothing or shoes.

Simple Activities with One Object

The following activities are frequent and widely varied at all ages:

- Exploring (carefully, usually with one finger)
- Palpating
- Giving (to the observer)
- Lifting up
- Opening (book)
- Picking up
- Pulling
- Pulling at nipple of the baby bottle
- Pushing
- Putting back or straightening (an object that fell or was turned around)
- Putting down
- Rubbing
- Scratching
- Shaking
- Shutting (book)
- Squeezing
- Taking from one hand into the other

Activities with Several Objects

The activities comprise the following:

- Aligning, putting next to (e.g., the toy broom next to the spoon)
- Balancing (e.g., the mirror on the pot)
- Pressing with (e.g., the plate with the nipple of the baby bottle)
- Putting into (e.g., the mirror into the pot)
- Putting on top of (e.g., the book on the pot)
- Putting together, assembling (e.g., baby bottle, cloth, and mirror in a heap)
- Putting the nipple back onto the baby bottle, or trying to do so
- Pushing (e.g., the mug with the spoon)
- Rubbing (e.g., the carpet with the spoon)
- Tapping or beating (e.g., on the brush with the spoon)
- Touching (e.g., the book with the spoon)
- Turning (e.g., using the spoon to turn the beaker around)

Interpretable Activities

As defined before, these are activities that either show that the child knows the conventional use of an object, or that the child is "pretending." The following activities enter into this category:

- Brushing with brush (own hair, doll's hair, teddy bear's fur, clothes, or other object)

- Caressing (dolls, teddy bear)
- Cleaning doll's or teddy bear's bottom with cloth and/or sponge
- Cleaning an object with sponge and/or cloth
- Dressing or undressing (dolls)
- Dusting with feather duster
- Feeding (oneself, dolls, teddy bear with spoon, plate, etc.)
- Getting the doll to eat (putting the spoon into her hand)
- Holding the mirror toward the face of the doll or the teddy bear
- Hugging (dolls, teddy bear)
- Looking at doll's pants before or after it has been put on the potty-chair
- Looking at self in the mirror
- Paging (through the book, looking at pictures)
- Pouring (from baby bottle into beaker)
- Putting on potty-chair (dolls, teddy bear)
- Putting handle of spoon to bottom of doll or teddy bear
- Putting the mirror into the hand of the doll, so that she can look at herself
- Putting to bed (dolls, teddy bear)
- Rocking (dolls, teddy bear)
- Sweeping with broom
- Washing (with sponge or cloth on own face)
- Washing (with sponge or cloth on doll's face)

Illustrations and Discussion of Developmental Periods

The observations show some clear developmental trends. A division into two periods seems to be justified: (1) from 10 to 18 months and (2) from 18 months on. The first period is well within the sensorimotor stage of intelligence, whereas the second inaugurates the stage of representational thought.

From 10 to 18 Months

At the ages when our observations started (i.e., 10–12 months), infants already possess many action schemes; their manual and postural mastery allows them to act with comparative ease on the objects at their disposal. Similar actions to those in the two other studies were observed.

By the end of the first year (and maybe already a little before the age at which our earliest observations were made), a certain dissociation between the action itself and the object used has already taken place. On the one hand, a single scheme is applied to several objects; and on the other, a single object is successively manipulated according to various schemes.

This phase is well illustrated by the example of Ch. at 12 months (see p. 154). During the first minutes of the observation session, when he applies two activities (taking and throwing; taking and putting on something else) to various objects (spoon, bottle, doll, mirror, plate, beaker, pot); during the third minute, Ch. manipulates the feather duster in numerous ways (it is shaken, used to beat with on the floor, explored by hand, put into the pot, thrown away).

Another example is provided by L. at 12 months. He takes the plate, rubs it against the wall, throws it, feels it, takes it up again, lifts it, throws it, takes it up again, throws it again. Later, he takes the spoon, rubs it against the plate, raps with it on the plate, and so on. During 15 minutes, L. practices several action schemes: beating, rubbing, turning around, and throwing, and he is clearly very pleased with his own activity.

From the age of 12 months on, a differentiation similar to that noted in the other two studies is observed. The spoon is often used in the same way as a stick (i.e., to push with or to pull things closer). The sponge is squeezed with the help of other objects. The nipple of the bottle is pulled and pushed inside the bottle, and there are efforts to insert the handle of the brush into the bottle or to push the spoon inside the bristles of the brush, and so on. But, with the materials used in this study, these behaviors do not develop into experimentation or fabrication of new objects; they become differentiated in accordance with the conventional usage of the objects presented. Certain activities of this phase resemble those observed in the study reported in Chapter 1: Objects are put into the beaker or the plate, and they are put next to or on top of one another. But, instead of developing into the prelogical activities of Chapter 1, these activities develop (1) into the collecting of objects that belong to familiar scenes (meals, housework, dressing, washing, etc.), (2) into the use of these objects in the conventional way, and (3) into pretend play.

During the first months of this period, activities that indicate this type of development begin to appear. They seem to constitute a kind of transition toward the clear conventional use of objects and toward genuine symbolic pretend play. Despite their often fugitive character, and despite the difficulties of interpretation, two types of transition activities can be distinguished:

1. A beginning of delayed imitation and thus of conventional action

2. A beginning of meaningful groupings of objects that the children know belong to familiar, regular happenings in their daily life.

It is often very difficult, however, to decide whether an action really does belong to one of these transitory types. For example, when a child manipulates the hairbrush; turns it around in all directions; beats with it against the wall, then against the floor; taps with it on the plate; and suddenly, briefly, passes it along the back of his head, is it justified to interpret this last action as either the conventional act of brushing hair or as an imitation of what the child has seen somebody else do earlier in the day?

Similarly, when a child brushes his or her face with the hairbrush, is this to be considered a badly adjusted movement, or is the child trying out the feeling of the bristles against his or her cheeks? Many such behaviors were observed and noted as "ambiguous." Some are carried out on one object. When children feel the face of the teddy bear, are they interested in the soft feeling of the fur, or are they caressing the bear? When they pull at the dress or the pants of the doll, are they undressing the doll or feeling the cloth? Other such activities are carried out with several objects: When children rub the plate with the spoon (but without putting the spoon into their own mouths or in the mouths of the dolls) what is their intention? When a child brushes the carpet with the hairbrush and dusts the doll's face with the feather duster, there is certainly a beginning of habitual usage (the brush is used for brushing, the duster for dusting), but the actions are only partly conventional.

Activities of putting objects together are often equally ambiguous. Yet, intuitively we had the impression that around the age of 14–15 months, children start intentionally putting together some of the objects used for eating (spoon, plate) and somewhat later the objects used in housework (broom, duster). Collecting objects to do with toileting appears later (see Table 3). Usually, these collections are not exhaustive; only very occasionally do older subjects collect all the eating utensils before starting a well-elaborated play scene (e.g., mealtime for the dolls).

Some of the activities we observed resemble the "ritualized play activities" noted by Piaget (1946/1962), such as the following (Piaget, 1946/1962, Observation 62).

(J.) pulled her pillow from under her head, and having shaken it, struck it hard and struck the sides of the cot and the doll with it; as she was holding the pillow, she noticed the fringe, which she began to suck. This action, which reminded her of what she did everyday before going to sleep, caused her to lie down on her side, in the position for sleep, holding a corner of the fringe and sucking her thumb. This, however, did not last for half a minute and J. resumed her earlier activity.

In such behaviors, schemes are translated into action without an adaptive purpose and take no effort to learn—they are simply "played." At this level, however, it is not yet possible to discern in the child's behavior an awareness of pretending or "doing like Mommy." The sketchy actions of scraping the plate or of brushing are, in fact, performed out of context (it is not the proper time or place for a meal or for getting dressed), but they do not seem to be intentionally playful and are often clumsily carried out.

Thus, it appears that before the child becomes capable of intentional pretend play, there is a transitional period during which objects belonging to familiar scenes are assembled and imitative actions are sketchily performed out of context.

From around the age of 15 months, the activities become organized in such a way that the observers no longer hesitate to regard the children's activities as intentional, conventional, and correctly carried out. Among these activities, which we have called "interpretable," the following two types can be distinguished:

1. The child uses in an adequate and conventional way one or several objects: He or she dusts with the duster, sweeps with the broom, cleans with the cloth, pages through the book, and so forth. Apart from looking at the picture book, all the other activities are performed outside their real context and often imply the evocation of an absent object (there is no food on the plate, no dirt to be swept

up). Similarly, the children carry out actions on themselves—putting spoon in their mouth, saying "mmmm," looking at themselves in the mirror, and so on.

2. The children handle the toys that represent living creatures (dolls, teddy bear) in an adequate manner. First, they handle them without attributing an active role to them: They hug the doll, rock the teddy bear, and so forth. Later, it becomes clear that these toys are considered to be active partners in more complex play episodes: The child brushes the doll's hair, undresses it, and puts it on the potty-chair.

Table 3.3 shows the number of children at each age that were observed to engage in such activities. For the period under consideration, Table 3.3 shows that

- Interest in the mirror is evident at all ages and remains constant. Before the age of 13 months, however, it is difficult to decide whether children are really looking at themselves or whether they are simply interested in this shiny object.

- The conventional use of most of the objects (the first 6 items in the table) is observed from the age of 12 months on.

- "Behaving as if one is eating" is the earliest observed pretend activity.

- Dolls and teddy bear are recognized as replicas of living beings. They are hugged and kissed, and toward the end of this early period, they begin to assume a more active role.

At the end of the sensorimotor period, a knowledge of familiar objects has thus been acquired that is sufficient for these objects to be used in a conventional way outside of the

Table 3.3

Ages for Participation in Activities

Age in months	10/11	12	13	14	15	16	17	18	19	20	21	22	23	24	25–27
Sweeping		1			1	3	4	2		1	4	6	5	2	
Brushing		1	1	2	3	2	3	5	6	4	4	2	2		4
Dusting		1		1	1	2	7	1	1		6	4	1	3	5
Paging book			1	1		4	4	3	3	2	4	3	5	3	4
Cleaning or dusting				1			1		1	1	2	2		1	1
Looking in mirror	2	4	4	5	5	4	5	6	6	5	7	4	5	5	5
Feeding oneself			1	2	2	3		3		2			2		
Washing oneself			1								2	1	1	1	1
Rocking	1									1		1		1	
Feeding		1			3			1		3	5	3	1	1	3
Caressing		1		1				2		1	1	1		1	1
Hugging			1		3	4	4	4	3	6	1	5	1	1	4

Activity	Values
Brushing hair	1 3 1 2 3 2 1 1 1 4 1 3 5
Putting doll on potty	1 1 1 1 1 1 1 1 1 5
Kissing	1 2 2 1 1 1 3 3 3
Dressing, washing doll	1 1 2 2 4 5 2 2
Putting to bed	2 1 5 1 5 3 3
Undressing	2 3 1 3 3 3 5
Presenting mirror to doll	1 1 1 1 3 1 3
Spanking	2 1 2 1
Looking at pants	2 2 2
Pouring	2 1 1
Adjusting nipple	1
Stick into bottom	1
Spoon into bottom	1
Making doll feed herself	1
Brushing exp.'s hair	1

normal context. This acquisition may appear trivial, but it is the result of a lengthy development during which action schemes are transformed into meaning-bearing actions ("signifying actions," in Piaget's terminology). In this progressive differentiation of the objects according to their daily use, the contribution of imitative behavior is evident. For example, it would seem impossible for children to succeed in performing the complex activity of brushing their hair by direct coordination of action schemes or by apprehension of the physical properties of the brush. A hairbrush seems a typically conventional object, the function of which is impossible to detect except by observing other people's behavior (in contrast to a mirror, the conventional use of which can be discovered by exploration). These activities do not yet constitute symbolic behavior in the strict sense because they do not necessitate the evocation of absent objects or events. However, they surely prefigure the various later forms of such symbolic acts. Similarly, putting together the duster and the broom, the mirror and the brush, or the spoon and the plate are acts that prefigure the later search for attributes common to a set of objects.

At the same time, as the activities become more precise in their meaning, they also become better organized spatiotemporally, in line with the stages of sensorimotor development described by Piaget. I. Lézine and I. Casati's development scale was applied to all our subjects within a few days of the session in which they were observed in our experimental situation. This scale was established on 305 children between the ages of 6 and 14 months (Lézine & Casati, 1969), and it confirmed the sequence of stages derived by Piaget from observations of his own three children.

By the age of 7 months, children have gone through the first three stages:

- Stage I: elementary sensorimotor adaptations or reflex adaptations

- Stage II: primary circular reactions

- Stage III: intentional sensorimotor adaptations or secondary circular reactions.

Stage IV starts at about 8 months and lasts until 11–12 months. During this period, a coordination of schemes and their application to new situations starts. For example, when presented with a new object, the child now applies already acquired schemes (e.g., take, rub, shake) as if trying to understand the new object. At this stage, the infants begin to explore objects more and more actively and intentionally; great progress is observed in the choice of means to realize a desired goal. Our youngest subjects were either in this or the following developmental stage.

Stage V goes beyond previous acquisitions, beyond the application of well-tested means to known or unknown situations. From stage V on, the child begins to be able to invent new means in more complex situations, and to show unforeseen behavior. For example, the child discovers, by trial and error, the mechanisms of the opening of a box; she or he actively looks for an object that has disappeared in front of her or him by taking into account what was seen of its previous movements; after numerous trials, she or he discovers how to use an instrument in order to grasp an object desired; and so on. The various efforts are already well directed, but success is only reached after a series of attempts. Stage V is that of tertiary circular reactions and the discovery of new means through active experimentation.

With stage VI (starting between 16 and 18 months), the child becomes capable of inventing new means of reaching a goal by mental combinations, which lead to a sudden understanding or insight and make multiple trial and error superfluous. At that time, the transition between sensorimotor intelligence and representational intelligence has started.

In our observations, at the time when the infants show the first action differentiation, 50% of them have reached the end of stage V, and 50% are at the beginning of stage VI.[1]

When the activities become more precise and better adapted to the conventional use of the objects, 80% of our

---

[1] In each stage, there is a distinction between behaviors that characterize the beginning and those that characterize the end of the stage.

subjects had reached the end of stage VI (i.e., the transition period between sensorimotor behavior and behavior that shows the beginning of the symbolic function).

From 18 Months to 2 Years

The main difference between the observations made with infants below the age of 18 months and with those above that age is the fact that the latter's activities begin to form sequences and are coordinated in much longer episodes. The sequences are also more and more frequently inserted into a meaningful framework that the children construct from their daily experiences.

This progress is clearly illustrated in our protocols by the behavior of the children with the figural toys (i.e., toys that represent people or animals themselves capable of acting) dolls and teddy bear. Before 18 months, these toys were manipulated infrequently, and then mostly to tap on them, push them, throw them, feel them, put them upright. But after 18 months, sequences of interpretable actions occur when the child hugs or pets the dolls or the teddy bear while still treating them as passive partners.

A. *at 19 months,* for example, takes the teddy bear, hugs it, holds it against her face, puts it in her lap. Then she takes the doll, hugs it, turns it around several times, puts it in a sitting position on the floor, picks it up and hugs it, kisses it, then puts it back down on the floor.

A few months later, children begin to explore the body of the dolls (and of the teddy bear).

P. *at 22 months,* for example, spends several minutes feeling the head of the baby doll, exploring its eyes with his forefinger, pulling its foot, putting his finger into its ear, pulling on its apron, turning it around several times, and so on.

Simultaneously, the first play episodes in which the figural toys are made to play a more active role are observed. For example, the children often put the spoon into the mouth of the doll, brush its hair carefully, and so forth.

These activities will develop further along two lines: In the first place, the children become capable of setting up a situation in which a sequence of precise actions is carried out in the course of one complex activity.

P. at 22 months, for example, acts out a complete scene of a mother feeding her baby. He puts the nipple of the baby bottle against the lips of the doll, with a clear and precise gesture, while he holds the doll in his other arm, curved around its body, lifting its head with his hand. Then he holds up the bottle, pulls on the nipple as if it were stuck, looks at the bottle, shakes it just like an adult feeding a baby and checking the level of milk in the bottle. Then he gives the bottle back to the doll and pushes the nipple strongly against its mouth.

A little later, another scene of similar complexity is also played: cleaning, wiping its mouth, and dressing the doll after having fed it.

In the second place, the same scene is often played first with one of the figural toys, then with the others. The children brush and clean the doll, then the other doll, then the teddy bear; or they feed the dolls and then the bear.

Still later, from about 24 months on, dolls and teddy bear become active partners in the play episode. For example, the children put the doll in front of the plate and put the spoon into the doll's hand, as if it could eat by itself. Or, when they brush the doll's hair, they put the mirror into its hand so that it can look at itself (earlier on, they held the mirror in front of the doll's face after having done its hair).

Still later, the children's behavior clearly and frequently indicates their evocation of absent objects. They start using substitute objects: For example, the child tears bits of the piece of paper and puts them onto the plate so that the doll can have something to eat. Or they evoke absent objects by their own actions: The child picks or scoops something up from the floor and brings his curved hand toward the mouth of the doll.

From $2\frac{1}{2}$ years on, symbolic play episodes become more and more elaborate, and the children are able to construct scenes that take up the total observation session, with the dolls and the teddy bear all taking part and even interacting among themselves. These highly elaborate and long-lasting sequences are not, however, observed with children of the age range concerned in this study.

Children's Awareness of Their Own Bodies

Activities on the child's own body, with or without an object, and their relation to the activities carried out on the dolls and the teddy bear were analyzed separately by Lézine (1976–1977) in view of their intrinsic interest.

Phases in the early awareness of the child's own body have often been described by those who observed very young infants. Bühler and Gesell provide many analyses of exploratory behavior of infants a few months old. Wallon, with the collaboration of Lurçat, carried out many research projects on body image, postural space, and environmental space, but with older children. Similarly, many tasks on body knowledge and orientation in space have been designed and used with children from 3 years on. By contrast, the period between 12 months and 2 years has not been investigated much.

In our study, it was possible to observe activities carried out by the children on their own bodies, as well as activities carried out on the body of the doll. The activities are first reported separately, and then their relationship is discussed.

Children's Activities on Their Own Bodies

As indicated earlier, exploratory activities using an object have been distinguished from those performed with the hands only.

Exploration by Means of Hands

Though our subjects were encouraged to use the objects in front of them, it still happened, especially during the first minutes of the observation sessions, that they withdrew; if so, they often began to explore their own bodies. It also happened from time to time that activities with objects were interrupted by such explorations. We do not intend to discuss postures, gestures, and facial expressions because they were not inventoried systematically, nor were discharge movements of the head, trunk, arms, and legs, or other circular reactions. However, because the study of these movements might well contribute to our understanding of the successive stages in the participation of the body in interaction with other people, they surely merit close attention.

Here only some aspects of the activities on the infants' own body are reported, particularly those in which hands (without an object) are used to feel, scratch, or strike parts of the body. The frequency of activities in the oral zone and on different parts of the head (ears, nose, eyes, cheeks, scalp, etc.), arms, legs, the axial region of body symmetry, chest, belly, and genitals was noted (apart from one subject of 19 months, who scratched the back of his neck, no subject showed any interest in the back, shoulders, shoulder blades, or buttocks).

The inventory shows that *oral activities* (sucking of fingers or hand, which is known to take place during the first hours of life and even in utero) are the most frequent between 10 and 24 months. Doubtless, these activities satisfy a deep-seated need, as well as serve exploratory and experimental purposes (container–content problems).

Apart from these very frequent activities, the following were noted the following:

- *Putting hand(s) on knee(s).* Probably the child derives some autostimulating pleasure from palpating this salient part of the body, which, moreover, is easily available. Whenever the child is sitting down, with the legs bent, the knees, with their rounded surface, are prominent. Similarly, it has been noted that palpation of knees appears at about 4 or 5 months, whereas palpation of feet—more difficult to reach —does not occur before 6 or 7 months.

- *Putting hand between the legs.* The children explore not only their genitals, which often are difficult to touch because of clothes, but also the body's axis of symmetry and the empty space enclosed between their legs.

- *Putting fingers in nose.* An exploration of orifices.

- *Putting hand(s) on the feet.* The feet are mobile parts of the body that can be moved by hand, as well as independently. They are relatively far removed from the hands. In Wallon's opinion, the child considers them to be autonomously existing objects up to a certain age. Wallon gives the example of a child taking a bite out of a biscuit and then offering it to his foot. Many such behaviors were noted in our observations; the children frequently brought the spoon, the mug, or the baby bottle to their feet after bringing them to their mouths.

- *Putting hands to eyes.* Often this takes the form of rubbing the eyes, an action that apparently relieves feelings of unease.

- *Bringing hand(s) to ear(s).* Ears, like knees, are salient parts of the body.

- *Putting hand(s) on hair.* Infants often begin their exploration of the mother's body by grasping her hair, a very primitive act, which, according to certain authors, constitutes a residual reflex activity. Similarly, infants explore other orifices (mouth and eyes) and salient parts such as the nose. Breastfed infants often close their mouths on their mother's nose.

It is interesting to note that the hand, the prime instrument of exploration, is itself little explored. When the infant squeezes one hand with the other or entwines, twists, or pulls his fingers, these activities are often the result of a state of tension. None of the subjects ever carried out a finely adjusted and continuous palpation of a hand, such as was often observed of a foot.

In our observations, no differences were found between girls and boys regarding the frequency of the contacts between the different parts of the body and the hands.

Exploration by Means of a Handheld Object

It might be supposed that the use of a tool (an object that acts as an intermediary) to touch certain body parts would modify the topography of exploration, but, curiously enough, the landmarks of discovery remain almost the same whether the children are holding an object or not.

The following activities were noted:

- Oral zone activities are dominant; the objects are brought to mouth, they are sucked, rubbed against the lips and bitten.
- The legs are frequently touched and tapped with an object.
- Objects are often put on the knees.
- Certain objects are used to touch the face.
- The feet are rubbed or tapped with various objects.

Objects are used to touch the extremities, the head, and the hands. Exploration of ears, forehead, and back of neck is rare and occurs late; the back of the neck is only touched by the hairbrush during brushing activities from about 15 months on.

The choice of objects to be brought into contact with certain parts of the body seems to reflect a certain understanding of their function.

For example, the objects most often brought to the mouth to be sucked, licked, or bit all belong to the set of eating utensils (bottle, mug, spoon). The objects most often brought to the face are the mirror and the hairbrush. They are also used to touch the head. Only rarely are they used to touch other parts of the body. This reinforces the hypothesis that the infants are beginning to know the conventional use of these objects from the age of 12 months on.

Activities with Figural Toys

Three of the objects given to the infants in our study suggest a correspondence with the child's body-image: a child doll with long hair that opens and shuts its eyes and has mobile arms and legs, and a mobile head; a small doll (hereafter called "baby") without any hair; and a teddy bear. All three are about the same size. The child doll and the baby doll are dressed in underpants and dresses; the child doll wears shoes.

At all ages, and at whatever the initial distance of these objects from the child, the protocols show a much greater frequency of manipulation of the child doll than of the baby doll or the teddy bear.

Among the activities of the children with these toys that relate to knowledge of the body, the following types can be distinguished:

1. Bringing the toys into contact with the child's own body;

2. Exploring the body of the dolls or the teddy bear. These explorations are meticulously and systematically performed, and, among the older infants, they are often accompanied by verbal commentaries.

3. Activities that have been called "signifying" and pretend-play and that are produced in sequences, such as first brushing the doll's hair and then playing at feeding it.

Bringing Toys into Contact with the Child's Body

These activities are often the following: hugging one of the figural toys, pressing the toys against their own belly or face. The teddy bear is most often the object of a search for contact with something soft. The bear is brought to the face, held against the belly, squeezed under an arm. These activities are most frequently observed between 15 and 19 months.

Difficulties of interpretation often arise. Is the child particularly sensitive to the softness of the teddy bear's fur? Does the child possess a similar toy at home, to be showered with affection, a behavior that is perhaps reinforced by the family? If so, the teddy bear can function as a consoling object (transitional object) that gives the child an outlet for emotional upsets. Or does the child consider the teddy bear to be alive? When the children hold the bear and hug it (it is softer than the dolls), do they feel that they get a response or a reinforcement of feelings of contact? Or do the children imitate attitudes of their mothers? Many more observations are needed to elucidate these points, but the general line of development can be illustrated by the gradual emergence of symbolic play in the activities of a little girl who is very attached to the teddy bear (she plays almost exclusively with the bear).

H. at 16 months takes the teddy bear, pulls its ear, turns it around, squeezes it against her belly, pulls on one of its legs, squeezes it against her chest, rocks backward and forward with the bear held against her.

At 19 months, she takes the bear by its paw, gets it to sit down. It falls and she laughs. She takes up the bear again, hugs it against her, gently feels its head.

At 20 months, she takes the teddy bear, shakes it joyously, laughs, says "titi bébé" [little baby], holds out the bear toward the experimenter, gurgles, shakes the bear, babbles, screams with joy, says "nounou mé" (nounou = bear), hugs it hard, looks at it, speaks to it, pinches its face, pulls the ribbon it has around its neck, and starts to rock it, then pulls its ear, shakes it, hugs it.

At 22 months, H. takes the teddy bear, puts it in her lap, laughs, says "hop-là" bouncing it on her knees, explores its eyes with her forefinger, pulls its ear, clutches the bear against her face, takes it by its ear and says "Oh, mon nounours" [Oh, my bear], then bends down and kisses the bear.

Exploring the Bodies of Dolls

These activities involve detailed and systematic exploration of different body parts: The child touches or scratches gently with the tips of the fingers, several times; the child may use the end of the feather duster or the broom, the handle of the spoon or of the brush, or the mirror; the children also sometimes explore with the palms of their hands.

Exploratory activities on the baby doll and the teddy bear (both less articulated than the child doll and with less clear facial features) are mainly carried out on the extremities (head and feet), the middle region (belly), and the eyes. Such activities are far more frequent with the child doll, and concentrated on its eyes, hair, and feet. Until about 18 months of age, exploratory activities are rare and remain associated with simple schemes such as throwing, turning, and tapping or beating. For example,

P. at 15 months touches the foot of the doll, pushes it, throws it, takes it up again, pulls its hair, turns it around, shakes it, balances it holding it by its head, beats it with the spoon.

Sometimes the children seem to compare the child doll and the baby doll. For example,

A. at 15 months grabs the doll by a foot, puts it down in a sitting position, pulls its hair, puts it on the plate, puts his hand on its head, shakes it, swings it by its foot without looking at it, then looks in turn at the child doll and the baby doll, pulls on a foot of the baby, turns it around, pulls the head of the baby, puts it down, takes up the doll by its head, feels it, turns it, and pulls its hair. All these activities are done slowly, and the child holds the toys either by the head or by a foot.

From 18 months on, the exploratory activities become more precise and better localized. They are often carried out with the forefinger and accompanied by attentive looking. For example,

V. *at 18 months* touches a foot of the baby, explores its eyes with her forefinger, touches a foot of the baby, explores its eyes again, pulls it toward herself, touches its head, explores its eyes, touches its feet, explores its eyes, picks it up and explores its eyes, and repeats this sequence over and over again.

L. *at 20 months* puts her forefinger into the mouth of the doll, lifts up its hair and puts her finger into its ear, then puts her finger into its eyes, then pulls the eyelashes.

Beginnings of Pretend Play

The first episodes concern daily experiences, such as dressing and undressing the figural toys; meals with the aid of the spoon, the baby bottle, the mug, and the plate; putting the doll to bed and placing a blanket (a piece of cloth or paper) over its legs; or brushing its hair, holding the mirror in front of its face. In certain activities, use is made of a substitute object, such as putting a stick to the bottom of the doll to take its temperature and saying "she is ill." Or the child mimes the presence of an absent object, pretending to pick up something and holding it in front of the mouth of the doll saying "eat!" The actions are well localized on the body of the dolls; simultaneously, the actions on the child's own body become more skillful.

Interest in the doll's eyes, mouth, and hair goes together with apparent interest in its head and feet; however, the extremities are obviously the points where the toy is grasped most easily. Between 12 and 18 months, the children take the dolls by their head or feet indifferently; the toys are sometimes held with the head downward. At later ages, the doll is always held with its head upward, vertically or slightly inclined, except when the children turn them around, take off their underpants or spank them. Exploration of the back of these toys is rare, except when the doll's dress is unbuttoned (observed 15 times), when its pants are pulled down to put it on the potty-chair (12 times), or when it is being spanked (8 times).

An instance of a lack of differentiation between back and belly is provided by one child of 21 months old, who first explored the baby's face slowly and systematically, then its feet, then turned it around to undress it and to spank it, and then turned it several times beating repeatedly its back and its belly in turn.

Relations between Activities on the Child's Own Body and Activities on the Dolls

It is interesting to compare the way the children carry out simple gestures on their own bodies (putting the spoon into their mouths, brushing their hair with the hairbrush, holding the mirror in front of their faces and looking at it) with the way they carry out similar actions on the dolls. How does the transition from actions on one's own body to actions on another's body take place, and when do these actions become easy to carry out without any hesitation?

In our observations, clumsy gestures appear first both on the child's own body and on the dolls, and only later do gestures become adequate. For example, when brushing their own hair, the children sometimes bring the brush to their cheek or forehead. They may also tap on their head with the brush, or the brush may be held with the bristles pointing away from the head, though otherwise correctly used. Later, the children brush their hair smoothly, holding the brush in the proper way.

Similarly, the youngest children sometimes bring the spoon toward their face, head or ear, without reaching their mouth. Later, the spoon is immediately brought to the mouth and placed between the lips. The mirror is sometimes put against the head, the hair, or an ear or a cheek, but later it is held in front of the face in the appropriate position.

Smooth and correct execution of these actions demands both mastery of movement and knowledge of one's own body. The difficulties the children encounter when acting on their own bodies they also encounter when acting on the dolls.

Developmental Sequence

Analysis of the data shows the following development:

From 10 to 13 Months

During the first period, the children pay no attention to the dolls, and many bring brush, spoon, and mirror toward their own head or face, and tap or rub with them. About half the children already show well-adjusted movements with these objects from the age of 12 months on.

Between 15 and 18 Months

The children carry out the actions on their own bodies with progressive mastery and show sporadic interest in the dolls. However, the hairbrush is more often used to tap on the head of the doll than to brush its hair.

From 18 Months On

The children are able to brush the doll's hair correctly, to hold the mirror in front of its face, and to put the spoon into its mouth. These activities are frequently interspersed with the same activities on themselves, as if they still needed the reference to their own body.

From 20 Months On

The children are able to brush their own hair, to put the spoon into their own mouths, and to look at themselves in the mirror with well-adapted and precise gestures while carrying out these actions on the dolls, without any hesitation. For example;

L. *at 13 months* brings the spoon to his mouth, turns it around, brings it to his hair, beats his head with the spoon, smiles.

G. *at 17 months* brings the spoon five times to his mouth after scraping the plate with it, then points the spoon at the doll's forehead.

M. *at 20 months* brings the spoon several times to her mouth after dipping it into the mug. She then directs the spoon toward the mouth of the doll and immediately afterward brings it back to her own mouth.

Between 18 and 24 Months

The children engage in detailed and repetitive explorations of the bodies of the figural toys. They systematically explore the bodies of the dolls and the teddy bear and make frequent comparisons between the toys and their own bodies.

R. *at 18 months* touches the ear of the teddy bear repeatedly, then the doll's ear, then his own.

G. *at 18 months* touches his foot, pulls his sock, touches the foot of the doll, tries to take off its shoe, examines his own foot.

L. *at 19 months* caresses his own hair, then the doll's hair, and again touches and pulls his own hair.

C. *at 20 months* brings the bottle to her mouth, then to her
    foot, then presses it on the baby's foot, then on the
    foot of the doll.

From 23 months on, such activities are directly carried
out on the dolls without hesitation. Sometimes the children
start to act on the dolls and then come back to their own body.
For example,

J. *at 24 months* takes the doll, lifts up its hair, brushes its hair
    and holds the mirror correctly in front of the doll's
    face so that the doll can look at itself. Then she
    brushes her own hair and looks at herself in the
    mirror.

By the age of 2 years, children are thus able to do
without references to their own bodies and to act directly on
the dolls (which they have earlier explored and often manipulated). In general, it appears that between the ages of 1 and 2
years, children begin to know their own body through repeated actions that give them pleasure or that relieve a state of
tension. These actions start with the exploration of the extremities and of the salient parts of the body. There is, at first, little
interest in the middle part of the body. Also, hands are
privileged instruments of exploration and are more rarely
explored than feet. The same stages are found in the exploration of the dolls and of the teddy bear. Before the age of
18 months, children tend to take their own body as reference when exploring the figural toys. After this age, they
directly explore the body of the dolls and the bear, at first
with poorly adapted gestures, later, around the age of 2 years,
often during symbolic play, with precise gestures that imply
knowledge of the different parts of the body and their function.

As an example, longitudinal protocols on two infants,
Christophe and Pierre, are presented in the following (noted
minute by minute):

Observation 1: Christophe

At 12 Months

1. Throws spoon—keeps still with arms extended—throws bottle[2] (lh)—looks at obs.—touches doll, touches bottle—throws doll—throws mirror—throws plate—puts mirror on plate—

2. puts spoon on plate—takes up spoon—turns mug around—puts it on plate—throws mug on plate—throws spoon—turns plate around—turns pot around—throws it—puts plate on pot—looks at obs.—

3. throws plate—shakes duster—beats on floor with duster—throws it, touches spoon, looks at duster—holds it out toward obs.—turns it around in his hands—rubs it on floor—takes pot (lh)—puts duster in pot—throws duster—

4. turns pot around—throws it—throws mirror—crawls toward duster—throws it—crawls—turns around—shows mug to obs.—puts brush[3] into pot—puts brush into mouth—turns it around—whines—holds the brush out toward obs.—

5. brings brush to mouth—puts it in pot—brings it to his mouth again—throws it—rubs duster on pot—puts it in pot—throws pot—takes duster (lh) and broom (rh)—

6. lifts up broom—taps on broom with duster—listens to noise produced—throws broom—looks at obs.—throws broom—turns broom around several times—throws it—throws brush—takes baby[4] by foot and throws it—looks at obs.—

---

[2] Bottle = toy baby bottle; lh = left hand, rh = right hand

[3] Brush = hairbrush

[4] Baby = small doll.

7. beats with duster toward the pot—puts mirror into pot—holds out mirror toward obs.—throws it—puts duster into pot—beats with duster—puts plate on top of pot—crawls toward bottle—crawls toward and takes book—puts bottle on book—stays on all fours and looks between his legs—

8. walks on all fours—falls—shakes bottle—brings it to his mouth—puts it on book—brings it to his mouth, wrong way round—turns it around and brings it to his mouth—

9. pulls nipple—brings bottle to mouth wrong way round—puts it into his mouth—taps on book with the bottle—crawls away with bottle in mouth—is startled by a noise (bottle falls)—puts bottle back into mouth wrong way round—turns it around—pulls on nipple—

10. looks at obs.—rolls bottle on floor—puts it into mouth—bites it—looks at obs.—bites it—bends—bites bottle at other end—turns around completely—loses bottle—

11. puts plate on pot—holds plate out toward obs.—puts it on pot—crawls away—takes plate away from pot—throws it—puts duster into pot (lh)—puts plate onto pot—throws pot—

12. holds out duster toward obs.—rolls pot—screams—holds out duster toward obs.—throws it—brings bottle to mouth—(obs. puts him back in a sitting position on the floor)—beats with the broom on the pot—throws it into the pot—turns it around—throws it—

13. crawls toward piece of paper—throws sponge—brings sponge to mouth—throws it—crawls away—throws cloth—tears paper—shakes the duster—presses it on the paper (obs. puts him back in sitting position)—puts paper in mouth—taps with duster on floor (lh)—

14. throws broom—holds duster out toward obs.—taps with mirror on duster—brings mirror to mouth—throws mirror—pulls on feathers of duster—crawls away—throws teddy bear—throws spoon—pulls carpet—crawls away.

At 14 Months

1. Puts brush next to mirror—throws both—shakes bottle—pulls nipple—brings bottle to mouth—throws it—touches plate—beats on plate with spoon—then on mug—puts spoon into mug—says "eh"—looks at obs.—puts spoon again into mug—says "tè tè"—

2. puts spoon down into mug—rubs plate with spoon—puts spoon again into mug—says "ah"—looks at obs.—puts spoon again into mug—says "mam ah"—throws mug—gets up—walks away—taps with spoon inside mug while walking—

3. puts spoon into mug—crawls—gets up—looks at obs.—sits down—puts spoon into mug—gets up—goes toward door—babbles—taps mug with spoon—crawls—puts bottle into mug—puts bottle into mouth—

4. goes toward obs.—bites bottle—looks around—pulls off nipple—puts it down—crawls—gets up—tries to put nipple back—brings nipple to mouth—crawls away backward—turns around—crawls—rolls mug on floor—puts spoon into mug—throws spoon—(obs. puts nipple back on bottle)—

5. brings bottle to mouth—looks in front of him—goes toward door—brings mug to mouth—throws it—throws book—brings bottle to mouth—bites nipple—puts mirror on plate—bites nipple—

6. (obs. puts him back into a sitting position)—throws book—takes baby bottle and pulls nipple—bites nipple—pulls off nipple—looks at obs.—says "hein"—taps with mirror on plate—throws mirror into pot—puts mirror on plate—

7. feels sponge—taps with mirror on pot—throws paper—puts mirror into mug—shakes it—puts mug upside down on plate—puts pot on plate—holds plate toward obs.—puts mug on plate—taps with mirror on plate—walks away and falls down—

8. puts plate on pot—says "tia"—puts plate on pot—beats floor with broom—throws it—gets up and walks around with plate and pot—

9. walks and holds plate securely on pot—goes toward the other end of the room—walks all around still holding plate on pot—comes back and puts pot on plate—holds doll out toward obs.—taps with pot on plate—puts pot on plate—walks around with pot on plate—

10. beats plate against pot—goes to other end of the room—falls—puts plate on pot—gets up—walks with plate and pot—says "hein"—walks all around—beats with broom against wall—throws broom—goes to other end of the room—

11. (obs. puts him back in a sitting position)—puts plate on pot—throws plate—crawls—taps with plate on floor—puts plate on pot—puts spoon into mug—puts spoon on plate—puts mug into pot—puts plate on pot—says "am"—

12. beats on floor with mug—puts spoon into mug—stands up—goes toward obs.—holds out mug—says "tiens" (i.e., there)—goes away beating mug with spoon—walks beating spoon with mug—takes broom—taps with spoon on broom—

13. gets up—gets down on all fours—takes plate—moves away from toys holding plate and spoon against himself—bites spoon—walks with spoon in his mouth—goes toward door—smiles—says "hein"—babbles, looking toward obs.—

14. walks on all fours—bites spoon—taps on plate with spoon—

15. crawls—puts spoon into mouth—takes it out—taps plate with spoon.

At 15 Months

1. Takes bottle and pulls nipple—puts bottle on plate—beats on bottle with spoon—takes mirror and taps on

plate with mirror—looks around—beats on plate with
mirror—beats with spoon on mirror—looks around
vaguely—beats on plate with mirror and spoon
together—takes bottle—lets go bottle—beats on mirror with
spoon—looks around—

2. looks at obs.—beats on spoon with
mirror—chews—throws doll—taps on his leg with
mirror—takes brush and puts together brush, spoon, and
mirror—takes brush and brushes his own hair (sketchy
gesture)—throws brush—takes up brush again and brushes
his hair adequately—looks at obs.—throws brush—

3. puts spoon and mirror on plate—throws spoon on
brush—takes bottle—with the other hand puts mirror back
on plate—pulls nipple of bottle—presses bottle on
mirror—takes mirror and looks at himself in the
mirror—licks mirror—turns bottle around, several
times—examines bottle and puts it in his mouth—takes it
out and looks at it—puts it back in his mouth—chews it—

4. puts mirror on plate—puts bottle on plate—looks at
obs.—brings bottle to his mouth—throws bottle on
plate—brings bottle to his mouth—pulls nipple off
bottle—puts bottle into mug—tries to replace nipple on
bottle—turns bottle around—throws nipple into mug—

5. gets up—throws bottle into mug—throws spoon into
mug—throws mirror into mug—takes out spoon and throws
it—takes mirror and presses nipple on mirror—replaces
nipple in mug—throws spoon into mug—throws bottle into
mug—throws mirror into mug—

6. throws spoon into mug—turns it around inside
mug—lifts up mug—takes spoon, bottle, mirror, and nipple
out of mug—puts nipple into mouth and bites it—throws
nipple—puts bottle back into mug—brings nipple to
mouth—chews nipple—taps on mug with spoon—

7. takes up bottle, examines it—presses bottle in
mug—looks at obs.—turns bottle inside mug—bends
over—takes sponge and lets go—

8. takes bottle out of mug and brings it to his mouth—puts bottle back into mug—puts sponge into mug—puts spoon into mug—takes sponge out of mug and puts it back—presses sponge on plate—beats on plate with spoon—beats on plate with mug—looks around vaguely—takes baby and lets go—puts doll on plate—takes it off—

9. shakes mug on plate—puts bottle in his mouth and chews it—looks at bottle—puts bottle back in mouth and chews it—looks at obs.—bites bottle—turns it around—looks at obs.—puts bottle into mug—looks at obs.—

10. puts bottle into mug—then puts spoon into mug—pulls doll by the hair—throws her—puts bottle in his mouth—bites it—bends over—throws sponge—takes out nipple that had remained in his mouth—looks at obs.—(obs. puts nipple back on bottle)—puts bottle in his mouth wrong way round—

11. bites bottle energetically—takes it out of mouth—looks at it—puts it back into mouth—puts mirror on plate—puts bottle on plate—puts mug on plate—then bottle on plate—then mug on plate—pushes plate away—throws pot—

12. brings mug to mouth—puts mirror into pot—puts pot on plate—lifts up pot—takes away mug—puts it on plate—puts pot on plate—lifts up pot—puts mug on plate—puts bottle on plate—

13. turns pot upside down—beats with pot on plate—covers pot with plate—wriggles his feet—

14. crawls toward book—looks at book—puts bottle on book—puts mirror on book—taps on book with bottle—then with mirror—puts bottle in his mouth wrong way round—keeps it in his mouth—crawls toward duster—crawls toward broom—looks at obs.—

15. feels duster—turns it around—turns broom around—rubs broom with duster—taps on broom with duster—beats duster against floor—then broom, held upside

down, against his own body—beats on floor with
duster—taps on broom with duster—becomes excited—beats
on book with duster, faster and harder—lets go of
everything and crawls toward obs.

At 19 Months

1. Pulls at nipple of bottle and bites it—looks at obs.—takes
nipple off bottle and tries to put it back—sighs—(obs. puts
nipple back)—takes nipple off again and tries to put it
back—looks at obs.—puts bottle down—takes brush and
brushes doll's hair with brush wrong way round—adjusts
nipple on top of bottle—

2. puts down bottle—looks at duster—takes and throws
nipple—takes duster and dusts floor (well-adapted
gesture)—takes spoon and rubs it against plate—

3. tries to put nipple back on bottle—folds his legs beneath
him—puts nipple back on bottle—puts down bottle—looks
at all the toys—takes bottle—pushes on it—brings nipple to
mouth—pulls off nipple and tries to put it back on
bottle—looks at obs.—puts down bottle—takes
sponge—throws it away—

4. dusts floor with duster—feels the feathers—tries to
insert feather in bottle—takes up nipple again—tries to put it
back—shoves bottle into nipple—sighs—puts nipple against
top of bottle—

5. tries to shove bottle into nipple—presses bottle—puts
nipple on bottle—presses bottle—puts nipple in
mouth—throws it away—puts nipple into pot—turns over
the pot—

6. throws away the pot—tries to put the nipple on the
bottle—presses the bottle—(obs. puts nipple back)—pulls off
the nipple—looks at obs.—stretches the nipple—

7. looks at obs.—tries to put the nipple back on the
bottle—introduces the end of the nipple the wrong way
round into the neck of the bottle—puts nipple in his
mouth—rocks to and fro—puts the nipple in the pot—puts

the bottle in the pot—throws the bottle away—picks up the bottle again and puts it into his mouth—picks up nipple again and tries to put it back on—

8. takes mirror—shakes it—turns it around several times—picks up doll by the hair and puts it in sitting position—brushes head of doll with mirror—and then with brush—puts mirror in pot—puts brush in pot—takes up mirror again and beats it against brush—puts brush on plate—brushes spoon with brush wrong way round—puts spoon in mug—then puts it in his mouth—

9. puts spoon into the mug and again into his mouth—then spoon into pot, brush into mug, spoon into mug—says "caca" [poo poo]—puts brush into mug—brings brush to his mouth—puts brush into mug—and then into his mouth—beats mug with brush—

10. puts brush on plate—then brush into mug—spoon into mug—spoon into mouth—spoon on plate—bottle to mouth—brush into mug—spoon into mug—presses bottle—beats his foot with bottle—rubs his foot with his hand—leans bottle on his foot—spoon on foot—

11. places bottle on spoon—spoon on plate—mirror on bottle—brings bottle to mouth—puts bottle in mug—brush into pot—brings bottle to mouth—sucks bottle for long time—

12. presses bottle—throws it away—dusts carpet with duster—turns pot upside down—throws it away—says "ah pipi" [pipi = pee]—puts pot on plate—throws pot away—taps with duster—taps with mirror—looks at himself in mirror—

13. beats plate with mirror—puts bottle on mirror—brings mirror to his mouth—takes duster—pulls out some feathers—then brushes carpet—bottle to mouth—throws duster—takes book—says "wa wa encore wawa"—

14. pages through book and looks at pictures—pages—looks—leans with both hands on book—throws book away—

15. touches doll—takes mug and says "encore wawa"—shoves mirror into mouth—brings mug to mouth—beats mug with mirror—puts mirror into mug—brings mirror to mouth—takes book—turns it around—throws away mug—says "a plu wawa a plu wawa" [possibly means no more drink].

At 24 Months

1. Takes bottle—pulls off nipple—tries to put it back on—turns around and says "bonbon qu'est c'est ça oh làlà" [candy—what's that?]—turns around—takes brush—says "balai, ça" [that broom]—looks at obs.—sweeps with well-adapted gesture—beats on the floor with the broom—sweeps again—stands up—

2. goes toward obs.—touches the microphone cable—looks at obs.—takes broom—and standing up, sweeps the floor very well—beats on his leg with the broom—sweeps again—puts down broom—takes the mirror and turns it around—looks at himself close up—goes toward obs.—

3. sits down—looks at obs.—looks around—shows broom to obs.—says "c'est ça le balai" [that's the broom]—sweeps very well—changes hands and sweeps with lh—says "oh là là"—

4. stands up—goes to touch a stool—picks up nipple—tries to put it back on bottle—goes toward obs.—says "oh y est cassé" [is broken]—tries to put the nipple back on—holds the bottle out to obs. who puts nipple on—

5. sits down—pulls on nipple, making a noise—turns bottle around—pulls nipple making a noise—looks at obs.—stands up—goes toward obs.—walks all around the room—sits down again when requested—

6. tries to put back nipple—stands up and touches microphone—refuses to sit down again—cries and says "veux voir tata" [want to see auntie]—stoops to pick up

book—says "veux voir tata"—walks all around the room—sits down again on request.

7. takes the pot—says "pot" [pot]—takes plate says "qu'est que c'est ça" [what's that?]—takes brush and very effectively brushes the hair of the doll—says "pas beau les cheveux" [not pretty hair]—says "bébé" [baby]—looks at doll—brushes it energetically—brushes head of baby—touches the bear—brushes bear effectively—

8. hugs bear—tries to shove handle of brush into neck of bottle—brushes bottom of bottle—pushes bottle into mug—brushes bottle—throws brush—

9. sits down—takes book wrong way round—pages through it—looks at pictures—pages with lh—looks at pictures—pages—looks at pictures—pages—looks attentively at one picture—shuts book and throws it away—gets up—sits down again—

10. takes duster—dusts floor efficiently—throws duster—takes spoon—puts down spoon—takes paper—folds and unfolds it—gets up and touches table—

11. sits down—takes paper—folds and unfolds it—looks attentively at paper—gets up and touches microphone—looks at obs.—says "veux voir tata"—says "bébé nounou" [baby bear]—sits down—brushes head of bear—says "y est pas beau le nounous non" [he's not pretty teddy no]—takes broom—says "tiens le balai" [there the broom]—sweeps well—shows brush to obs. and says "que c'est ça?" [what's that?]—says "t'as vu" [you see?]—takes broom and sweeps well—

12. puts down broom—gets up and goes to obs.—says "veux voir tata"—sits down again—takes bear and throws it away—throws away brush—throws mug—stands up—goes toward obs.—says "veux voir tata, c'est cassé ça" [see auntie, that's broken]—touches microphone—

13. says "y est cassé tata" [it's broken auntie]—then says "et ça tata" [and that auntie]—touches the microphone—(he is

brought back to the toys by obs.)—refuses to sit down—takes and throws the doll—picks up the book—holds it out to obs.—shows the picture on the cover—smiles—

14. opens the book—pages through it—looks at a picture and says "c'est là tata et ça viens voir" [there it is auntie and that come and see]—tears off a bit of paper—pages through book and says "oh joujou tata" "gateau tata" [toy auntie, cake auntie]—beats on book—chortles—pages through book and says "cayon tata, maman un cayon, gateau tata, les joujoux tata" [pencil auntie, mummy a pencil, cake auntie, toys auntie]—looks at a picture and says "ah va là" [oh there it is]—throws down the book.

Observation 2: Pierre

At 12 Months

Pierre attentively looks at everything around him.

1. Takes bottle (lh) and brings it toward plate—takes plate (rh) and fiddles with bottle in lh without looking at it—turns bottle over on plate and pushes with it on plate—turns bottle again after lifting it and presses it against the plate—lets go of bottle—takes plate (lh)—pushes it away—takes up brush (lh)—puts brush on plate—rubs brush with lh—puts brush on plate—rubs plate with brush held the wrong way round without looking at what he's doing—

2. looks around him while rubbing gently with brush on plate (lh)—puts down brush—takes broom (lh)—puts it down—takes spoon (lh)—changes hands, takes spoon in right hand—puts spoon on plate—rubs plate with spoon held upside down without looking at it—

3. changes hands, takes plate (lh)—turns it around—puts it between his legs—takes broom with one hand and plate plus spoon in the other—smiles—changes hands—rubs plate with spoon (lh) looking at obs.—takes spoon (rh) and rubs on plate—

4. turns spoon around several times—turns spoon on plate—lifts up spoon and rubs it with his hand—bends over toward duster—looks at it—takes duster and rubs plate with handle of duster—turns duster around—rubs plate—throws duster—

5. takes spoon and rubs plate with spoon (rh) and then with lh—looks at obs., perplexed—rubs the spoon on the plate without looking at what he is doing, mechanically—looks at obs. and beats on plate with spoon—rubs plate with spoon—leans on plate with one hand—

6. changes hands—takes bottle—puts it on plate—presses nipple on plate—tries to put bottle upright—

7. looks at doll—rubs plate—looks attentively at doll (as if he did not dare take it)—looks at obs.—turns round—puts down spoon—takes broom (lh)—holds it upright—looks at it—stays still—takes spoon—rubs it on plate (rh)—puts down broom—takes duster (lh)—holds it upright on plate—

8. lets duster fall—takes broom—rubs plate with broom—rubs plate with spoon (rh)—puts broom upright (lh)—rubs spoon (rh)—puts broom upright (lh)—rubs spoon with broom—puts down spoon—puts broom on plate—takes and puts down broom again—

9. beats with spoon—turns round—takes bottle—presses it down on plate—turns round and goes away on all fours under a table—is brought back to toys and encouraged—

10. takes doll by its foot—pulls—sets it upright—puts it on plate—takes it up again—puts it down to his left—goes toward baby—picks it up by its foot—then by its head—shakes baby—looks at it—swings it (lh)—then swings it by its foot—puts it in sitting position—turns it toward obs.—

11. feels head of baby without looking at it (rh)—puts it down—pulls it upright—takes it by its foot—lifts it—puts it down—takes it by its foot—puts it down—lifts it up—shakes it by its foot—

12. swings baby held by foot and then by head—puts it in sitting position—reaches toward plate (lh)—looks at obs.—stays still—pushes away baby, baby falls—

13. puts baby up again—undoes his shoelace—pulls on it—looks round—takes up broom (lh)—changes hands—takes duster (lh)—puts broom down and puts duster on plate.

At 14 Months

1. Brings bottle immediately to mouth of doll, clumsily—takes brush (lh) and brushes face of doll—puts spoon on plate (lh)—changes hands—brings spoon toward doll but fails to reach doll—taps with spoon on mirror—turns round—looks at obs.—holds out brush toward obs.—presses bottle on mirror—

2. taps on mirror with bottle—puts spoon on plate—presses bottle on mirror—presses bottle on foot of baby—turns baby around—looks at pants of baby—throws baby—looks at bear—

3. goes toward bear—takes up spoon—puts spoon on brush—beats on floor with spoon—goes to get brush—brings brush toward spoon—pushes spoon on brush—pushes spoon into bristles of brush—

4. changes hands—presses with the spoon on the bristles of the brush—strongly presses bristles with spoon—says "hé"—shoves spoon—brings spoon near brush—lifts up brush—

5. puts brush behind him—presses with spoon on back of brush—takes hold of foot of doll (with his lh)—says "ah"—

6. crawls—takes and throws the sponge—shoves spoon into the brush—takes and throws the doll—crawls toward the mug—chortles—brings spoon the wrong way round toward his mouth—with the spoon hits on the mug, which is upside down—presses the spoon on the brush—

7. hits baby with the bottle—puts the spoon on the brush—holds out doll to obs.—stays still—hits the bottom of the mug with the bottle—hits the mirror with the bottle—

8. chortles—puts the bottle between the legs of the bear—shakes the bottle—presses with bottle on the head of the baby—looks at obs.—scratches between his legs—stands up—falls—chortles—

9. says "cuya"—takes spoon—taps the brush with the spoon—presses with spoon on back of brush—parts bristles of brush with spoon—changes hands—complains—takes book—

10. says "cuya"—looks at pictures—looks at obs.—hits mug on book—hums "au pus ah ah"—looks at obs.—

11. crawls toward paper—shoves it away—takes mirror—looks at himself—sits—takes book—hugs it—puts book on mug—takes up mug—complains—turns round—takes spoon—takes mirror—looks at himself—takes brush—holds it out to obs.—presses with spoon on bristles of brush—

12. complains—presses spoon on his shoe—hits mug with spoon—stirs with spoon in mug—brings spoon to mouth—

13. puts spoon upside down into the pot—puts spoon into mug—brings spoon to mouth—turns spoon in mug—lifts spoon—puts spoon into mug—beats mug with spoon—complains—chortles—brings spoon to mouth—dips spoon into mug—complains—slides on carpet—brings spoon the wrong way round to mouth—puts spoon into mug—brings spoon to mouth—

14. Puts spoon in mug—complains—puts spoon the wrong way round into mouth—puts spoon into mug—puts spoon into mouth.

15. rubs eyes—puts spoon in mouth—looks at obs.—puts spoon into mug—complains—brings spoon to mouth—looks at obs.—puts spoon the wrong way round into mug—puts it into mouth.

At 15;6 Months

1. Takes bottle (rh)—takes spoon (lh)—lets go of bottle—looks at mirror—takes it—looks at himself—looks in front—shakes mirror—puts it down—takes sponge (rh) and presses spoon on sponge (lh)—lets sponge fall—pushes again with spoon on sponge, several times—

2. appears very interested by his activities—pushes sponge with spoon 8 times—tries to scrape plate with spoon and seems to pour from spoon on sponge—tries twice more—

3. stays still with spoon and sponge in his hands—seems to think—puts spoon on plate—then on sponge—presses strongly on sponge with spoon—puts spoon on plate—scrapes plate—pours something on sponge—pushes spoon into sponge—

4. taps on sponge with spoon—turns spoon around on sponge—looks round him—begins again to press spoon on sponge, 8 times—changes position of his hand while pressing—

5. pushes spoon on sponge 4 times—puts spoon on plate then on sponge—shuts his eyes—obs. encourages him to go on—begins again to push spoon into sponge—puts spoon on plate—presses spoon into sponge—

6. puts spoon back on plate—presses spoon into sponge—puts spoon back on plate—pushes it into sponge—puts spoon back on plate—suddenly brings spoon to mouth—pushes it again into sponge—brings spoon to mouth—

7. closes his eyes—taps on sponge with spoon—opens and closes his eyes—beats about 10 times with spoon on and next to sponge—presses spoon into sponge—opens his eyes and closes them again—with his eyes closed, presses spoon into sponge—opens his eyes—looks in the air—

8. closes his eyes—taps on sponge with spoon—opens and closes his eyes—beats with spoon on and next to sponge, about 10 times—presses spoon into sponge—opens his

eyes—puts spoon on plate—then on sponge—puts spoon on plate—then on duster—

9. taps on duster with spoon—taps on sponge with spoon—puts spoon on plate then on sponge—pushes sponge out of the way—takes spoon (rh) and puts it on plate—changes hands—puts spoon on plate again—takes bottle—

10. puts bottle on plate—takes it up again—pushes nipple on floor—pulls nipple—takes up spoon again—puts it on nipple—presses with spoon on nipple—

11. puts spoon on plate—then on nipple—then on plate—puts bottle on his right—takes spoon—presses spoon into sponge, 3 times—throws sponge and takes mirror—

12. puts mirror on foot of doll—takes brush—presses spoon into brush—puts brush down on floor and pushes spoon into brush—beats on brush with spoon—puts spoon on plate—puts spoon on bottle—presses on nipple with spoon—

13. puts spoon on plate—puts bottle on floor—takes mirror—beats on floor with mirror—throws down mirror—pushes spoon into brush—taps on brush with spoon—puts spoon on plate—puts spoon on bottle, pressing strongly on nipple—

14. rubs plate with spoon—presses spoon into brush—stays still—

15. puts spoon on brush—puts brush on plate—puts spoon on brush—brushes plate with brush—turns spoon around on brush—changes hands—taps on plate with spoon—puts spoon on plate—puts spoon in mug—puts spoon on plate—puts spoon in mug—puts spoon on plate—puts spoon in mug.

At 18 Months

Pierre is inhibited and recalcitrant. Vaguely fumbles with the objects.

At 19 Months

Pierre comes reluctantly, hangs onto obs. and cries.

1. Stays still and whines—(obs. hands him the bear)—stays still—looks askance—looks in front of him—rubs carpet with hand—stays immobile and complains—

2. obs. hands him a piece of candy—Pierre pushes obs. hand away—looks at toys and rocks to and fro—

3. takes bottle—throws it far away—takes mirror—holds it obliquely and looks at himself—turns mirror around several times—

4. examines mirror—holds it obliquely and looks at himself—changes position of mirror several times looking at himself in between—whines—looks at himself—looks at toys—whines—puts mirror down—

5. takes mirror—scratches it with forefinger (rh)—slides it under his bottom—pushes it under his right leg—takes it up again—puts it straight—slides it again under his leg—scratches it—complains more and more loudly—turns mirror in many directions—makes it slide on the carpet—scratches it—

6. holds the mirror obliquely on his leg—makes it slide on his leg—takes it up—turns it around—makes it slide on his leg—complains—lifts up mirror and looks at himself attentively—takes bottle—turns it around on mirror, 5 times—presses on mirror with bottle (rh)—

7. holds mirror obliquely and pushes bottle onto it—on one side and then on the other—and then on its circumference—starting from left to right and then from right to left—taps on mirror with bottle—

8. turns bottle around—pushes it on mirror—slides mirror on his leg—pushes bottle on his leg—complains—pulls up his shoulders—sighs—protrudes his mouth—looks around him—freezes totally—

9. complains—lifts up mirror and looks three times from close by at himself, bending his head—moves the mirror on his left leg—bad-tempered, he puts it down on the floor—

10. turns the mirror vaguely—slides it under his right leg—holds it obliquely and looks at himself—turns mirror—blinks—turns mirror—

11. presses bottle on his leg—gives a start—presses bottle again on leg—presses nipple strongly on leg—complains—coughs—pushes nipple on leg—

12. pushes nipple on leg—turns bottle—rubs ear (lh)—hunches and scratches his ear, rocking to and fro—

13. rocks while holding his body with his arms and pretends to sleep, pressing his cheek against his hand, while pressing bottle against leg, eyes closed—rocks—gives a start—rocks—pulls his head down between his shoulders and remains in this position for 2 minutes.

During this session, Pierre gives an excellent example of the use of defense mechanisms against a situation he dislikes, going so far as to simulate sleep. As soon as the observer comes to him and says "O.K. Pierre, finished, we'll go back to the others," he opens his eyes and begins to laugh roguishly. He now accepts the piece of candy he had refused before. He gets up gaily, takes the hand of the observer, and leaves the room. Did Pierre pretend to be asleep? Or was he really tired for a moment? It is impossible to know for sure.

At 22 Months

Pierre, in good humor, comes readily.

1. Takes baby—looks in the air—frowns—looks askance at obs.—looks at toys—

2. feels foot of baby—makes it sit—clasps baby against him—puts it down—looks at baby—takes it up again and makes it sit properly—

3. scratches baby's foot—feels his own socks—feels his shoe—and his socks—pulls the apron of the baby—feels its head—

4. looks askance—feels his sock, looks at toys—feels baby's foot—then its face—puts his finger into the eye of the baby—changes hands—touches his legs—palpates head of baby—then its feet—

5. palpates for a long time the baby's head—scratches the baby's feet—

6. palpates baby's head—looks at toys—

7. freezes, totally immobile—feels himself between his legs—touches his shoes—feels head of baby—changes hands—pushes both his hands on head of baby—

8. explores with his forefinger the eyes of the baby—pulls the baby's foot—swings the baby in the air—puts his hand into baby's underpants—pulls baby's feet—feels baby's face—

9. takes hand of baby—puts his finger into its ear—feels the baby's shoulders—lifts up the baby—turns it around—looks at the baby's pants—pulls on the baby's apron—

10. lifts up baby's apron and feels baby with his hands—beats baby's behind—pulls apron—

11. turns baby round and beats on its belly—pulls apron—turns baby around and beats its bottom—makes baby sit down—looks at doll—

12. takes doll—lifts up its dress—pulls on pants (lh), baring its bottom—beats its bottom—puts doll down—takes up baby—makes doll sit—

13. pulls pants of baby—beats its bottom—makes baby sit—takes doll—lifts up dress—beats doll's bottom—makes doll sit down next to baby—doll falls over—

14. makes doll sit again—takes baby—pulls on apron—beats on its belly—beats on its foot—bares baby's belly and strikes

it twice—beats foot of baby—puts down baby—pulls a thread of the apron—

15. takes bottle—puts nipple to mouth of baby skilfully—takes baby in his arm, holds its head—lifts up bottle—pulls on nipple, as if it were stuck—looks at bottle—shakes it (exactly like an adult who feeds a baby and checks the level of milk in the bottle)—gives bottle to baby, pressing nipple against its mouth.

At 25 Months

1. Crosses his hands, holding one with the other—looks around—palpates and pulls on his fingers—looks at toys—pulls his shoe—opens his hands and shakes them—touches himself between his legs—palpates his foot and pulls it—

2. pulls his sock—feels his knees—looks around vaguely—bends over—feels his socks—bends—touches the brush with his forefinger—

3. pushes brush with his forefinger—pushes down on handle of brush, making the other side go up as a lever—feels the bristles—touches bottle—takes it and lifts it up—

4. takes mirror and looks at himself—looks around—looks closely at himself in the mirror—palpates mirror—brings it toward his face and looks closely at himself—turns mirror around several times—looks at himself—changes hands—

5. turns mirror around—rubs his mouth with handle of brush—palpates mirror—yawns—turns mirror around and around—brings mirror to his mouth—shakes it—takes sponge—

6. touches doll—takes bottle, turns it around—palpates nipple—takes brush and feels bristles—changes hands—presses on brush—

7. palpates brush—scratches with both hands—turns it around and around—looks around—brings brush toward

him sliding it on the floor—pulls mirror toward him and looks at himself—

8. touches inside his nose—puts his nasal mucus on mirror—rubs his fingers—looks at himself—puts mirror on mouth of doll twice—holds doll in correct position so that it can look at itself, holding the mirror obliquely and looking at how the doll looks at itself—

9. takes mirror and looks closely at himself—turns mirror around and around—looks at himself—looks at obs.—looks at himself—brings mirror again toward face of doll—puts bear upright and holds mirror in front of its face—bends over to see if bear can see itself and adjusts position of mirror—

10. puts mirror down—takes bear and makes it sit down—takes doll and feels its pants—takes baby and feels its pants—pulls pants of baby and puts it down—

11. takes doll and pulls pants—looks at doll's bare belly—pulls again on pants—takes baby and bares its belly—looks at belly of baby—puts baby behind doll—

12. scratches his head—puts baby on doll and adjusts baby's position so that it sits properly in doll's lap—bares baby's belly and beats it—brings bottle to baby's mouth—shakes bottle in the air and hits baby's head with bottle—puts mirror on baby's mouth—

13. puts bear on baby—takes bear and puts it on plate—presses bottle on foot of bear and then on its face—puts bottle on knees of doll—puts bear on baby—

14. rubs his nose—yawns—feels his knee—lifts up bear and smiles at it—takes baby away and yawns—pushes bear away—puts baby in sitting position on plate—

15. pushes bottle with mirror—puts doll that had fallen backward into sitting position on plate—puts brush next to bottle—puts doll against baby—takes book, pages through it, skillfully points to car in one of the pictures—says "toto"

[car]—pages again—looks for car—finds it—points at it and says "toto" while looking at obs.

At 26 Months

1. Twists his socks—looks around vaguely—bends over—looks at toys—scratches his calf—

2. looks around vaguely—twists his socks—looks around vaguely—beats on his foot—

3. bends over—touches mirror—turns it around—takes mirror and looks at himself—inclines mirror—sticks out his tongue, looking in the mirror—turns mirror around and around, holding it obliquely, and sticks out his tongue several times, laughing and looking at himself—takes bottle and pulls and then pushes down nipple—

4. pulls gently on nipple—pushes it down—pulls nipple—puts down bottle—takes brush and brings it immediately toward his hair, brushing the fringe on his forehead (rh)—brushes the hair of the doll—quickly holds the mirror in front of doll's face so that the doll can look—brushes hair of doll again (all done quickly and skillfully)—brushes own hair—

5. brushes head of baby—tries to take off doll's shoe—touches himself between his legs—puts doll down and pulls pants—tries to take off doll's shoe—bends over—pulls baby toward him—puts baby into sitting position—takes doll and makes doll lie down—

6. touches doll's foot with brush—puts spoon on plate—scrapes—pours something on foot of doll—takes duster and beats on foot of doll—puts down duster—takes broom and beats foot of doll with broom—turns broom around, scratches it—puts it down—looks at toys—sighs—takes bottle and presses on nipple—

7. pours from bottle into plate—beats on foot of doll with bottle—puts bottle back on plate—beats on foot of baby with bottle—twice—beats on foot of baby with broom—puts baby

in sitting position—and beats on its head with handle of
broom—

8. takes baby and makes it lie down—puts handle of broom
into baby's mouth—puts baby back in sitting position—puts
broom on floor—pushes broom—aligns broom and
duster—palpates his knees—takes doll and makes it
sit—makes doll lie down next to baby—

9. takes bottle and beats with it on baby's foot—beats doll's
foot with bottle—pulls nipple of bottle and gets it
loose—pretends to pours from bottle on foot of doll—then
on foot of baby—tries dextrously to put nipple back onto
bottle—pours from bottle onto spoon, then from spoon onto
foot of doll and then onto foot of baby—

10. pretends to pour from spoon into pot—takes bottle and
shakes it inside mug—pours from mug onto foot of doll and
then onto foot of baby—pours from mug on belly of baby
and then onto foot of doll—pours from bottle into
mug—puts bottle on plate—shakes nipple in mug as if
pouring something—

11. tries skillfully to put back nipple on bottle—puts nipple
on his finger (like a thimble) and brings his finger to neck of
bottle—pours from bottle onto his neck—wipes his neck
with hand—puts forefinger into neck of bottle—puts nipple
onto bottle—takes it up again and presses it on foot of
doll—puts nipple on plate—

12. pours from bottle into mug—then onto foot of
doll—pours from mug onto plate—tries to put nipple back
on bottle—pours from bottle into mug—presses nipple into
mug—shakes mug—throws nipple away—puts mug on foot
of doll—turns mug around and around—

13. takes mug—brings it to his mouth—puts mug
upside-down on plate—rubs mug on floor—puts lh into
mug—presses on mug with both hands—shakes mug—beats
on mug—rocks mug, holding it against himself—listens to
noise coming from another room and murmurs something—

14. puts nipple on bottle but wrong way round—brings bottle to his mouth—puts bottle in mug—pours from mug onto plate—brings mug to his forehead—puts doll on mug and looks with head on one side under the dress of the doll, as if to see whether the doll has wet its pants—turns doll around and feels pants—

15. puts his hand under doll's dress—pulls up dress and bares doll's belly—feels belly—sighs—yawns—takes mug and makes gesture of pouring liquid onto head of doll—puts doll on plate—pours from bottle onto foot of doll, then onto pants of doll turned around—takes baby—puts it on plate—explores pants with hand under apron—turns baby around—lifts up apron and puts hand underneath—pulls pants—puts baby down in sitting position—takes baby and puts baby on plate—puts doll on floor opposite baby, then takes doll and shakes it.

Concluding Remarks

In all the behaviors noted in this study, imitation of what other people do clearly plays an important part. During the observation sessions themselves, the children were essentially alone because the experimenter remained withdrawn, never interfering and never participating in the children's activities (even when the children asked for such participation). The behaviors observed must therefore have been elaborated in different situations, in interaction with other persons. The experimental situation does not reproduce the conditions in which the observed behaviors were acquired. This is no doubt the case in most other developmental psychology research, as well as research in other fields of psychology. For example, nobody believes that number conservation is elaborated by the child in daily life under conditions that resemble those of the experimental situation. Tasks that can be called "pure" (in the experimental sense) allow the experimenter to observe no more than the results of acquisitions attained in other circumstances.

However, the experiments have other advantages, notably that of allowing the psychologist to study various aspects of the concept under investigation in a single experimental setup.

One of the questions that may be asked concerning the present study is the following: How would the infants have acted with the various objects if they had been in the company of other children or of participating adults? This question can only be answered by further experimentation, and such an investigation was started by Musatti (1979) with children between 18 and 38 months. In general, Musatti's results confirm the developmental trends brought to light in our study, but they also show some interesting communicative aspects of the observed activities.

With our youngest subjects, the observed development followed that described by Piaget in terms of a double differentiation: On the one hand, objects become differentiated from actions and come to exist in their own right, acquiring particular properties of their own; on the other hand, the actions of the subject become differentiated from the actions of others. The first differentiation means that the child comes to understand that when he or she performs an action, he or she could have done another action on the same object, or the same action on another object. On the basis of the second differentiation, the child understands that what she or he did somebody else could have done too, just as she or he understands that others could do other things. Thus, when a child at this stage beats on the floor with a spoon, the activity is no longer felt to be an indissociable whole; such an action now implies a choice: taking a spoon *and not* a sponge (which would not make a noise), and taking a spoon *or* a broom (both of which make a noise). The spoon is now also apprehended as an object with which many actions can be performed: throwing it, beating with it, putting it into one's mouth, and so on.

Many of the early behaviors observed in our study (cf. the protocol of Christophe, 12 months, in the present chapter) illustrate the differentiation between object and action. The experimental situation did not allow behavior reflecting the second differentiation to be observed. The latter is evidenced by many activities reported by Piaget (1937/1955, Obs. 152 et seq.) indicating that, at that age, the child becomes aware of the fact that other people can do what he or she can do, but that they can also do things he or she cannot yet do (and vice versa). At this age, the child begins to give objects to another person in order to start a shared activity—that of giving and taking. Children no longer use the hand of another person as an instrument to be directed toward objects that are outside their reach; instead, they show what it is they want by pointing, by looking at a partner and vocalizing, and so forth.

The acquisitions of this double development have also been observed with the Lézine-Casati scale. The tasks that figure in this scale were originally designed by Piaget to serve as possible indications of how infants at this stage coordinate their actions in a coherent structure ("the group of displacements"), leading to the attribution of invariant properties to objects ("retrievability") and to an early structure of causality ("objectified and spatialized causality").

Clearly, the persons that live with the infant play an important part in this development: They will be the first objects from whom the child expects some regular behavior; they will also be the first retrievable objects, as they are also, in Piaget's words, "the first objectified sources of causality because, through imitating someone else, the subject rapidly succeeds in attributing to his model's action an efficacy analogous to his own" (Piaget, 1937/1955, p. 360).

We want to emphasize that this development evidenced by the results obtained on the Lézine-Casati scale goes hand in hand with the progressive mastery in the conventional use of objects. There thus exists in early cognitive development a contemporaneousness between (a) the attribution of "retrievability" and "permanence," which both are properties of all objects, and (b) the apprehension of particular properties, such as "used for hair brushing," "used for sweeping the floor," which are socially determined.

The conventional use of familiar objects simultaneously indicates (a) a knowledge of a particular object, derived from daily experience, and (b) a capacity for delayed imitation.

Conventional usage is only gradually mastered. We have seen that in early development, one of the objects may be used adequately, but not the other (e.g., the children indeed brush with the hairbrush, but they brush the floor and the legs of the doll as well as their hair). Only later will these objects be used altogether conventionally (e.g., the children sweep the floor with the broom, dust with the duster).

Only after the first conventional uses of familiar objects have been observed do the children show pretend behavior. It appears that knowledge about the social use of objects acquired through observation and imitation of what other people do opens the way for the construction of new processes. Imitative interaction provides social knowledge that, in turn, modifies the imitative activities: The latter can now be performed in the absence of the models, though at first not yet in the absence of familiar objects.

The observations allow us to establish a hierarchy of pretend activities: (1) such make-believe behavior has to do only with the children's own actions (pretending to be asleep); (2) the children engage in symbolic play in which objects are given a passive role (hugging or rocking objects), and, much later, (3) episodes of symbolic play are constructed in which make-believe partners play an active part (e.g., the doll is given a spoon so that it can eat; it is spanked because it has been naughty).

Thus, the development of pretend activities reproduces at a different level the development of the conventional use of objects; and this latter development goes hand in hand with that of delayed imitation. Symbolic behavior should, therefore, not be seen as something totally new, but as a higher-level restructuring of already acquired knowledge.

The analysis of body knowledge and of its parallel knowledge of the body of the doll is another example of such restructuration.

A further point has to be made. The reader may wonder where, in this study, the first verbal utterances, which have always been considered as the clearest signs of the appearance

of the symbolic function, fit in. We have many times empha-
sized that in our experimental situation, the children were
alone, for all practical purposes, which did not stop them from
performing numerous pretend-play activities. Moreover, these
activities are very similar to those noted at the same ages when
children are together (see Musatti, 1979). By contrast, verbal
behaviors are different. In our situation, the children only
very rarely vocalized or spoke.

The rare utterances observed either formed part of the
pretend-play scene or were addressed to the experimenter,
who gave no encouragement for further exchanges.

The rarity of verbal behavior in our situation is readily
explained in the light of recent studies on the acquisition of
language. Several authors wonder about the specificity
of verbal interaction compared to the various other, more
primitive forms of communication (Bruner, 1975; Snow and
Ferguson, 1977; Veneziano, 1982). From this point of view, it
seems possible that in language acquisition, specific factors
linked to communication intervene in interaction with the
elaboration of the type of signifiers described in this study. The
absence of communicative aspects from our situations makes
an interpretation of early verbal behavior impossible.

However, the development noted in the use of familiar
objects and in the pretend behaviors suggests two remarks.
The first concerns holophrases and two-word utterances. The
tendency to interpret these utterances as being made up of
nouns and verbs would seem to be erroneous. If delayed
imitation does indeed begin with the total integration of the
instrument–object and the action that is attached to the instrument, combined with a disregard for the object on which the
action is performed, the utterances that accompany such actions or utterances that call for such actions can hardly be
expected to make a distinction between action and object. The
second remark concerns the well-known phenomenon of over-
generalization (e.g., the child calls all men of a certain age
"daddy") and the, apparently constrasting, phenomenon of
overspecialization (the child calls only his own cat "kitty"). The

contemporaneity observed between the notion of the permanence of the object (a general property of all objects) and the knowledge of conventional usage (a property belonging to a particular object) suggests that both phenomena are aspects of the same nascent capacity of attributing meanings to objects according to the objects' intrinsic qualities.

General Conclusions

The three studies provided numerous data in answer to the questions raised at the outset. The infants' activities with the three kinds of objects suggest developmental lines for the logical or prelogical organizing of actions, as well as for invention and discovery.

In each of the three research studies, far-reaching changes were observed between the ages of 12 and 24 months in the course and succession of actions, in the questions the children ask themselves regarding the materials, and in the meanings they attribute to objects.

Some of the more noteworthy aspects of these changes are summarized, and a number of interpretations are proposed in the following.

Similarity and Progressive Differentiation of Activities

Up to the age of about 12 months, the observed activities are the same in the three studies, despite differences in the materials. In the Piagetian perspective, this is not surprising. The end of the first year after birth sees but the beginnings of a dissociation between action and object; the infant integrates objects into action schemes (simple and coordinated), and the physical properties or social significance of these objects are less important than the ease with which they can be used.

Clearly, however, because the activities are highly diversified, the properties of the objects do come into it to a certain extent. The fact that some objects are interesting to scratch, to use for beating on the floor, or to touch to one's face is not unconnected with their being malleable, rigid, or soft. In fact, in all three studies, the earliest differentiations that depended on the properties of the objects were observed at the age of about 12 months.

The earliest compositions of action sequences were observed at the same ages in all three studies: Either an action is repeated on different objects, or different actions are made to bear on the same object. Again, the beginnings of agglomerating several objects were observed at the same ages in all three studies: the infant creates envelopments and contiguities by putting objects into, on top of, or next to (touching) one another. The importance of *putting into* as a polyvalent source for the later elaboration of various kinds of knowledge appears clearly in these studies. Pursuing a purpose similar to ours, Forman (1973–1975) stressed the importance of *putting on top of* and *aligning side by side* (with contact), which were more frequent with his materials than with ours.

Creating envelopments and contiguities is often preceded by or followed by creating a similar relationship between an object and a part of the infant's own body. For example, before a rod is put into a cup, the rod may be put into the mouth, or the index finger may be introduced into the cup. Or before a ball of clay is placed on a cube, it may be placed on the subject's leg.

The use made of the objects presented for the research described in Chapter 1 (infants and logic) and Chapter 3 (infants and symbolics) shows the preponderance of *putting into*; the objects presented in Chapter 2 were less suitable for this purpose. In Chapter 2 (infants and physics), fragmenting occurs frequently, an activity that is rare in the other two. It should be pointed out, however, that with the materials of Chapter 3, the youngest subjects were often observed to scratch one of the objects or to try pulling the nipple of the bottle or the bristles of the brush, and these actions may in fact be unsuccessful attempts at fragmenting. As is the case for the activity of *putting into,* the activity of fragmenting appears to have great importance as a source of later elaboration of knowledge of various kinds.

The similarity of the activities of the youngest subjects in all three studies contrasts with the subsequent variety. At the age at which the observations came to an end (i.e., about 24 months), activities are very different from one study to the other. As was hoped at the outset, the three kinds of materials led to well-differentiated kinds of behavior.

With the objects of the first study (balls, rods, and either cubes or cups, with several of each, in graduated sizes), the following activities were observed:

- *Collecting:* Members of the same class of objects are put together in some special place. The infant collects all the rods or all the balls of modeling clay, or, less often, all the cups or cubes.

- *Nesting:* All the cups or cubes are put into one another, in descending order of size. These nestings are achieved via different strategies. The infant makes either nesting couples or nesting triplets before uniting the whole series, or the infant nests them one by one, concentrating on differences in size.

- *Making one-to-one correspondences:* The infant puts all the members of one class of object into relationship with all those of another class (e.g., putting a ball of modeling clay into each cup until the two series are exhausted).

The objects, though in themselves not very interesting, when presented several at a time, led to activities of a logical kind. It may be added that, while we expected the infants to collect and to nest the objects, the one-to-one correspondences came as a surprise.

With the objects of the second study (a tube, a piece of

spaghetti, beads, cotton wool, etc.), two main kinds of behavior were observed at 24 months that here have been called experimentation and fabrication, plus two other less frequent kinds of behavior.

- *Experimentation* is above all concerned with the movements of one object in relation to another (e.g., the infant introduces a stick into the tube, and by varying the position of the tube, he or she makes the stick slide out, holds it back by hand, or prevents it from falling out by holding the tube near the floor). Some essential activities of physicists seem already to be present in these behaviors: reproduction of an interesting event, verification of its regularity, variation of circumstances, and the discovery of new regularities.

- The *fabrication* of objects seems to spring from the act of piercing (e.g., when a rod or a piece of spaghetti is stuck into either a ball of clay or a ball of cotton, producing a combination of objects that does not of itself fall apart). The infants become interested in this new entity, add other elements to it (sometimes after having prepared them in advance, e.g., by fragmenting the stick of spaghetti) and give it a meaning. Often, they show another person the object they have made.

- *Tower building* and *parcel making* were rarely observed. The materials provided did not readily lend themselves to building. Parcel making, which combines *putting on* and *putting into,* was not observed before the age of 24 months. This activity gives rise to long sessions in which the child hides an object, finds it again, takes it out of its paper or cloth wrapping, and, in the end, packs it up again and gives it as a present to another person.

Fabrication, like parcel making, generally presents an element of make-believe or symbolic play, which brings these activities closer to those observed in the third study. The meaning given to a new object may sometimes be inferred from pretend behavior (e.g., the child blows at a stick with a piece of clay at its end as if it were a match).

The kinds of 2-year-old behavior observed with the materials of the third study (doll, teddy bear, familiar objects such as a plate, a spoon, etc.) are well known from many previous descriptions of play at this age.

- The doll and the teddy bear are treated as partners, and a scene is played, using real objects as well as symbolic objects that are absent (e.g., the doll is fed with the spoon, and the plate is scraped as if there were food on it). More rarely, the infants in our study conferred on an object a meaning that it does not ordinarily have (e.g., the doll is covered with a sheet of paper as if with a blanket).

Between the end of the first year after birth and the beginning of the third, there thus takes place a progressive differentiation of activities, depending on the objects available to the children. This differentiation goes together with the development of better coordination and longer action sequences in which the observer can more and more clearly make out the children's intentions and the meaning they attribute to objects and actions.

Is it possible in the three studies to discern some constants in the course of object-dependent differentiation? A number of characteristic features of the children's activities in all three studies have already been pointed out. Two of these activities—bringing together two objects (particularly putting one into the other) and fragmenting an object—seem especially fruitful as sources of new differentiations and coordinations.

The preponderance of these two activities is intriguing and recalls a passage in Piaget's autobiography (1976, pp 6–7). On the subject of his earliest writings he says,

> When reading them again . . . I am surprised to come across two ideas I still cherish and that have never ceased to guide me in my most diverse undertakings . . . the idea, which has remained central, that action contains

within it a form of logic and that logic, consequently, has its source in a kind of spontaneous organization of actions, (and secondly) that at every level—at the level of the cell, of the organism, of the species, of concepts, of logical principles, etc.—one encounters the same problem of the relationships between the parts and the whole.

The idea of action logic became one of the basic theses of genetic psychology. In this view, thought results from an interiorization of the organizing of actions, and knowledge is built up from sensorimotor ability or *knowing how*. This is one of the dialectical spirals that recur over and again in the works of Piaget: Actions with the *knowing how* inherent in them give rise to new knowledge, which, in turn, opens the way to fresh *knowing how*. As Cellérier (1979, p. 92) puts it,

> The activity resulting from the initial assimilation produces a change in the situation that brings out new features which in turn need to be assimilated by reconstituting, in terms of what is known, the practical and empirical or pseudo-empirical regularities associated with the new features. These "regularities" then constitute an acquisition that makes the up-to-date representation of the situation more specific, thus forming a new assimilatory setting by changing the preceding one.

It does not seem too hazardous to recognize in fragmenting and enveloping (or even in just bringing objects together) a concern of our very young subjects with one of the ideas cherished by Piaget (i.e., the problem of the relationships between the whole and its parts). In fragmenting, the whole is a continuous mass (cotton, modeling clay), which the child divides into parts (the progressive organization of this activity along two different approaches was observed), while in the activity of putting into (e.g., sticks into cups) a whole is constituted starting with separate elements. As was seen, these activities are very quickly followed by their reverse: The bits of cotton are stuck together again to form the original whole, and the objects put into the cup are taken out again. The problem of the relationships between the whole and its parts seems to be a vein to be followed in studying changes of activity between the ages of one and two.

The Whole and Its Parts

The relationships of the whole to its parts and of the parts to one another appeared to Piaget to be of capital importance, and it impressed itself on him as a pivotal idea "which would finally yield a close union . . . between philosophy and biology, and open the way to a truly scientific epistemology" (1976, p. 7). Because these activities are preferred, do the fragmenting of a continuous whole followed by its reconstitution and the combining of several objects followed by their separation play a similar pivotal role for 1-year-old infants? No claim is made that the activities observed in these studies are the only ones to play so important a role; it should be stressed once again that in these studies, only one child alone was observed at any given time and that consequently, the social aspect, if not totally absent, is very much reduced in importance in our studies. Nevertheless, within our limited scope, it does seem that the relationship between the whole and its parts leads to a number of more specific problems, and that the action schemes of fragmenting and enveloping (or, more generally, of combining) are a source of *knowing how* and *knowing that* in many different fields.

It is clear that action schemes are involved. An occasional action that is not repeated and that is not generalized by being applied to many objects is of course also based on a scheme. But, as our observations have shown, fragmenting and combining objects are indefatigably repeated, are applied to several objects, and are varied either by replacing one or the other of the objects (in combining) or by changing the actual procedure (in fragmenting), and they consequently must be regarded as typical schemes. What is more, toward the end of our observation period, the two schemes become coordi-

nated and indeed subordinated (the one—frequently, fragmenting—becoming a means in relation to the other). It may be
added that the two schemes in question, even at the age of our
youngest subjects, are complex and are the result of coordinations of earlier, simpler schemes.

Like all action schemes, those under discussion have
several aspects (or, as Piaget, 1980, p. 9, put it, several forms:
logical, spatiotemporal, and causal or physical). One or the
other of these aspects may dominate, depending on the focus
of attention of the subject and the problem she or he is trying to
solve, which in turn is dependent on the situation in which the
subject happens to be and the means at her or his disposal. The
younger the subject, the more the various aspects are merged
and the more his or her actions are dependent on the situation,
including the available objects. While all action schemes have
several aspects, it is also true that some action schemes are
richer than others, and it seems that the various logical,
physical, and spatiotemporal aspects are particularly interesting in the schemes of fragmenting (and reconstituting) and of
creating envelopments or contiguities (and of separating).

For the logical aspect, uniting and separating discrete
objects (one action being implicit in the other because putting
together certain objects means separating them from others)
and arranging objects (in its simplest form, aligning them
contiguously) are fundamental. This is true both for classification and for seriation, and a fortiori for their coordination
(i.e., one-to-one correspondences and number). What Piaget
calls "identification" (of an object by its insertion into an action
scheme) and "substitution" (by the insertion of a different
object in the same action scheme) leads to the domain of
differences and resemblances, the basis of classes and relations, the synthesis of which yields the number concept. By
making available to the infants a collection of nonfamiliar but
not very interesting objects in a number of replicas, a situation
was created in which the infants' attention was brought to bear
on their own actions and especially on the organization of their
actions.

In Chapter 1, we described the development of what, with Cellérier (1979), might be called new successive assimilatory settings brought about by action schemes that give new meaning to and provide new aims for activities: We described the changes that lead first from simple accumulations and localizations or individualizations to partial collections and distributions, and then to exhaustive collections and groupings, as well as to their coordination (i.e., one-to-one correspondences). Surely for the child, an accumulation of varied objects in a container has a different meaning from an exhaustive collection that no longer needs the material envelope of a container. But in both, the meaning must reside above all in the activity itself. What the children actually do—putting together and separating—remains the same, but meaning and aims change with age, and, for our oldest subjects, the same action has a different meaning, depending on the context. Putting all the cups into one another has a different meaning from putting all the cups (or rods) together, and putting a rod (or a ball) into each of the cubes has another meaning still. The final arrangements of the objects embody these different meanings, and prefigure the notions of classes, relations, and number without, obviously, the operatory coordination of extension and intension.

The development of action logic appears clear, and the highest point observed, at the age of about 24 months, seems to us to have as its origin the action schemes of putting into and of separating, dominated by the problems of relating the whole and its parts. The culmination of this progressive organization, as we observed it, is a form of *knowing how*, which, via a new series of assimilatory settings, prefigures logical concepts such as transitivity, classification, seriation, and so forth.

As regards the physical aspect of the activities, the action schemes of uniting and separating do not give rise to special developments that prefigure notions of physical causality (such as, for example, force and movement), but they lead to experimental procedures that provide a better understanding of reality. The difference seems to be due as much to the very nature of physical knowledge as to the state of our knowledge of how the child evolves notions of causality, a field about which less is known than about the evolution of logico-mathematical ideas. But in the domain of physics also, it seems reasonable to suppose that relationships between the whole and its parts, starting both from partitioning an object and then putting it together again and from actions of putting together and taking apart several objects might well be fundamental.

Indeed, a parallel development can be recognized in the research described in Chapter 2. With the objects used, the question of the whole and its parts is again at the fore, this time via the action scheme of fragmenting, as well as via the action scheme of *putting into*. With the ball of cotton, what dominates is fragmenting, followed by reconstituting the ball into a continuous whole. This action shows the special interest at a very early age in separating (gradually pulling out the cotton until a little bit of it becomes detached). *Putting into* frequently does not occur until a little later, probably because it is more difficult, because the objects did not include any ready container. Within the given situation, objects are put together by threading and piercing.

The first assimilatory setting is the introduction of one object (e.g., the stick or the piece of spaghetti) into another (e.g., the tube or the bead). Very quickly, the aim and the meaning of the activities shift from threading per se to the kinetic relationships between objects: envelopment and separation, and disappearance and reappearance. The new assimilatory setting is apparently experimental, with an explanatory aim.

Like threading, piercing starts in an assimilatory setting, with the practical aim of success in the action (e.g., sticking a rod into the ball of modeling clay). The next setting still has a practical aim, but with different meaning. The child creates a new object, which is an entity in itself and to which a meaning is attributed by analogy to a known object.

It is interesting to note the convergence between our observations of child behavior and the theoretical proposals made by Cellérier (1979, p. 92): "When the aim is practical, the cycle stops in a state of equilibrium once the activities organized in the initial setting encounter no further obstacles, whereas when the aim is explanatory, such a final setting does not seem to have a place in the sequence of events." When the aim is the practical one of fabricating a new object, "the cycle stops." When the aim is achieved, the infants actually do pause. By contrast, in experimentation, no such pauses were observed, but each discovery opened up new problems, thus extending the search for new solutions.

In the same research, we think we saw some development in the infralogical aspect of the action scheme of fragmenting (and reconstituting) a continuous whole. Fragmenting in the sense of actually pulling the cotton to bits seems to us to be related to the kind of fragmenting that consists in dividing the whole into parts *without* effective separation and that was observed with the string and the piece of spaghetti (which the infant shoves out of the tube bit by little bit). Although the link between such behaviors and the acquisition of the concept of measuring is less clear than the link between (a) collecting, nesting, and making one-to-one correspondences, and (b) logical operations, it does not seem to be going too far to attribute to these behaviors the meaning of marking the parts of a continuous whole, and it is indeed from such meaningful *knowing how* that the notion of measurement will evolve.

In the third study, developments rapidly take a different turn from what was observed in the other two studies, though the initial bases may be the same. After the period in which the different types of materials do not elicit differences in behavior, we observed activities that bear witness to a growing knowledge of events in daily life and of the use of familiar objects. In the early stages, these activities are sporadic and fleeting while the infants pursue activities resembling those noted in the other chapters. For example, the act of brushing one's hair may appear within an action series during which the infant pushes on the bristles of the brush, shoves the spoon into the sponge, presses on one side of the back of the brush as if it were a lever, and so on. Or, to give another example, putting the spoon in one's mouth and into the mouth of the teddy bear may appear in a series of *putting into* and *putting on top of*, in which objects are used that do not suit one and the same everyday activity. The meaning of these activities certainly changes once several of the objects used have a common everyday frame of reference.

We then observed the beginnings of symbolic play, in which an absent object is represented by gesture and related to the real objects by the general frame of reference. Later still, the frame of reference confers symbolic meaning to a substitute object that is used in a way far removed from its usual function. At the age of about 24 months, we above all observed snatches of scenes interrupted by other activities (e.g., Ch. sweeps, does something else, brushes the hair of the doll and the teddy bear, kisses the bear, does something else, uses the duster to dust, does something else, brushes the head of the bear, sweeps, does something else, etc.).

It was not until later that we observed symbolic play with several little scenes fitting into a scenario of a scope greater in meaning and time (e.g., an infant putting the doll to bed, having it get up again, doing its toilet, feeding it, etc.). In outline, such a broader setup was observed with P. at 26 months: P. washes, dresses the doll, feeds it, gets it to pee, puts it to bed, and so on, but the action is still dispersed.

Without wishing to strain the comparison, it does seem that the third study again has to do with a transformation of the assimilatory setting, as well as with the relationships between the whole and its parts. But in the development that leads to symbolic behavior, the relationship seems to consist in the creation of progressively larger frames in which the various bits of pretend play (already removed from reality) are inserted like parts of a symbolic whole. For example, brushing the hair of the doll as an isolated act does not have the same meaning as doing so within a whole scenario. It is perhaps admissible to believe that imaginative creation consists in constructing new meanings within an original meaningful setting.

Inverse Actions

While we have underlined the question of relations between the whole and its parts as being inherent in the action schemes of putting together and of fragmenting, we also underlined that these activities are soon combined with their inverse: taking objects out of the container, and thus separating them again, and then reconstituting the fragmented whole. This seems to be another important lead: The simple *knowing how* will later evolve into reversibility, a piece of *knowing that*, the importance of which no longer needs demonstration. For Piaget, reversibility is the essential feature of operations, and it seems to us that our subjects' interest, observed even at the earliest ages, in actions that recreate the status quo ante is one of the important aspects of our research.

It is also tempting to place in this same evolutionary line the children's investigations into double roles, which were observed at an astonishingly early age and were stressed many times in our descriptions of behavior. In the research of Chapter 1 as much as in that of Chapter 2, the infants were fascinated by the fact that an object used as a container could also be used as content, and that an object that moves relative to another can be held still while the other object is made to move relative to it. These double roles expressed in action seem of considerable importance on the logical level on account of the transitivity of relations, just as much as on the physical level on account of the succession of causal links. At the ages of our subjects, this double relation becomes manifest by attributing two complementary roles in successive actions to the same object (content and then container; an object that separates itself from another and then an object from which another one separates). This *knowing how* will only much later be transformed into knowledge that makes it possible to simultaneously attribute two complementary properties to one and the same object.

A parallel can be traced with the question of the whole and its parts: *Knowing how*, by its very nature, because it covers activities extending in time, is subject to the constraints of temporal succession. The transformation of *knowing how* into *knowing that* calls, among other things, for both a detachment from temporal succession as regards logic, and an understanding of the role of time as regards physics.

In this respect also, the third study differs from the other two, which is not surprising, given the special nature of make-believe and symbolic play. We were nevertheless tempted to compare the first use of substitute objects with inverse actions.

Many authors have reflected on the hypothesis that symbolic play makes a special contribution to mental development. G. Bateson (1972) underlined the importance in play of what he calls "metacommunication." He refers to a child playing the part of a dog, for example, who pretends wanting to bite someone playing the part of a cat and who transmits a message of the type "I, as a dog, am going to bite" but at the same time gives to understand that "It's not a real bite because I am not a real dog." Sutton-Smith (1971) gives a more precise formulation and attributes a specific role in cognitive development to play. He suggests that notions of quantitative conservation are prefigured in "the conservation of imaginary identities in play, despite the presence of contrary stimuli."

Without wishing to go as far as that, we believe that it is not overdaring to seek a link between, on the one hand, the children's interest in the double role of certain objects and in inverse and reciprocal actions, and, on the other hand, the beginnings of substitute objects being used in play, such as making use of a sheet of paper, for example, as if it were a blanket, or a stick as if it were a spoon. Here again, one sees the attribution of a different status to the same object, no longer via successive actions, but via a meaningful act applied to an object the child knows well and on which, by his action, he confers properties normally belonging to another object.

In make-believe, we also see a link with the relation between the whole and its parts, just as in the other two studies: the meaning "spoon" is attributed to a stick if it is within the general setting of "the doll's dinner".

So, beyond the period when the infant's activities were the same in the three studies, we find common sources of development in the fields of logic, physics, symbolics, and imaginative creation. The progressive differentiation and coordination of the infants' activities, the infants' investigation into new problems leading on from those they have already dealt with, and their capacity to attribute ever-new meanings to the objects and to the actions they exert on the objects are certainly also essential ingredients of their creative imaginative capacities.

Finally, we wish once more to emphasize a feature we think is of capital importance for psychologists and educators alike—namely, the tenacity and intellectual coherence the infants evinced when facing the problems they themselves raised and the meanings they themselves attributed to events. Their capacity for sustained concentration, which is manifest in a series of actions within a defined setting and lasts for the whole duration of our observation sessions, clearly shows that the "lack of attention span" and "brief concentration" attributed to children are but artefacts arising from observations made in situations that are foreign to the children's preoccupations. The very many opportunities we had of observing that the problems they concentrate on are in no way trivial or superficial but, on the contrary, profoundly scientific, creative, and discovery-oriented did not fail to surprise and delight us all along.

References

Bateson, G. (1972). A theory of play and fantasy. In G. Bateson (Ed.), *Steps to an ecology of mind*. New York: Balantine.

Beth, E. V., & Piaget, J. (1966). *Mathematical epistemology and psychology* (W. Mays, Trans.). Dordrecht, The Netherlands: Reidel. (Original work published 1961)

Bruner, J. S. (1975). The ontogenesis of speech-acts. *Journal of Child Language, 2*, 1–19.

Brunet, O., & Lézine, I. (1965). *Le développement psychologique de la première enfance* (2nd ed.). Paris: Presses Universitaires de France.

Casati, I., & Lézine, I. (1968). *Les étapes de l'intelligence sensori-motrice*. Paris: Editions du Centre de Psychologie appliquée.

Cellérier, G. (1979). Structures cognitives et schèmes d'action. *Archives de Psychologie, 42(180)*, 87–106.

Forman, G. E. (1973–1975). *Transformations in manipulations and productions performed with geometric objects: An early system of logic in young children*. Final report, University of Massachusetts.

Forman, G. E., & Hill, F. (1980). *Constructive play, applying Piaget in the preschool*. Pacific Grove, CA: Brooks/Cole.

Forman, G. E., & Kuschner, O. S. (1977). *The child's construction of knowledge: Piaget for teaching children*. Pacific Grove, CA: Brooks/Cole.

Gréco, P., Inhelder, B., Matalon, B., & Piaget, J. (1963). *La formation des raisonnements récurrentiels*. Paris: Presses Universitaires de France.

Inhelder, B., Ackermann-Valladao, E., Blanchet, A., Karmiloff-Smith, A., Kilcher-Hagedorn, H., Montangero, J., & Robert, M. (1976). Des structures cognitives aux procédures de découverte. *Archives de Psychologie, 44(171)*, 57–72.

Inhelder, B., Lézine, I., Sinclair, H., & Stambak, M. (1972). Les débuts de la fonction symbolique. *Archives de Psychologie, 41(163)*, 187–243.

Inhelder, B., & Piaget, J. (1979). Procédures et structures. *Archives de Psychologie, 47(181)*, 165–176.

Inhelder, B., Sinclair, H., & Bovet, M. (1974). *Learning and the development of cognition* (S. Wedgwood, Trans.). London: Routledge and Kegan Paul.

Kamii, C. (1975). *La connaissance physique: Une application de la théorie Piagetienne au préscolaire.* Genève: Rapport Polycopie, Université de Genève.

Kamii, C., & DeVries, R. (1979). *Physical knowledge in preschool children.* Englewood Cliffs, NJ: Prentice-Hall.

Lamb, M. E. (1977). A re-examination of the infant social world. *Human Development, 20*, 65–85.

Langer, J. (1980). *The origins of logic: Six to twelve months.* New York: Academic Press.

Lézine, I. (1976–1977). Remarques sur la prise de conscience du corps chez le jeune enfant. *Bulletin de Psychologie, 327(30)*, 3–9, 253–263.

Lézine, I., & Casati, I. (1969). *Les étapes de l'intelligence sensori-motrice.* Paris: Centre de Psychologie appliquée.

Lorenz, K. (1941). Vergleichende bewegungsstudien an anatinen. *Supplement, Journal of Ornithology, 89*, 194–294.

Musatti, T. (1979). Modalités d'échanges et organisation des actions de "faire semblant" dans une situation de jeux symboliques. *Cahiers du SRESAS, 19*, 165–208.

Nicolich, MacCune L. (1977). Beyond sensori-motor intelligence: Assessment of symbolic maturity through analysis of pretend play. *Merrill Palmer Quarterly, 23(1)*, 89–99.

Overton, W. F., & Reese, H. W. (1973). Models of development: Methodological implications. In W. Nesselroade & H. W. Reese (Eds.), *Lifespan developmental psychology and methodological issues.* New York: Academic Press.

Piaget, J. (1952). *The origins of intelligence in children* (M. Cook, Trans.). New York: International University Press. (Original work published 1936)

Piaget, J. (1955). *The construction of reality in the child* (M. Cook, Trans.). London: Routledge and Kegan Paul. (Original work published 1937)

Piaget, J. (1962). *Play, dreams and imitation in childhood* (C. Gattegno & F. M. Hodgson, Trans.). London: Routledge and Kegan Paul. (Original work published 1946)

Piaget, J. (1975). Etudes d'épistémologie génétique, *Equilibration des structures cognitives* (Vol. 33). Paris: Presses Universitaires de France.

Piaget, J. (1976). Les sciences sociales avec et après Piaget: Hommage publié a l'occasion du 80e anniversaire de J. Piaget. *Revue Européenne des Sciences Sociales, 14(38/39)*, 1–43.

Piaget, J. (1980). *Recherche sur les correspondances.* Paris: Presses Universitaires de France.

Piaget, J., Grize, J. B., Szeminska, A., & Vinh Bang (1968). *Epistémologie et psychologie de la fonction.* Paris: Presses Universitaires de France.

Piaget, J., & Inhelder, B. (1964). *The early growth of logic in the child* (E. Lunzez & D. Papert, Trans.). London: Routledge and Kegan Paul. (Original work published 1959)

Snow, C., & Ferguson, C. (1977). *Talking to children.* London: Cambridge University Press.

Smith, P. K. (1974). Ethological methods. In B. Foss (Ed.), *New perspectives in child development.* New York: Penguin Books.

Stambak, M., Barrière, L., Bonica, L., Maisonnet, R., Musatti, T., Rayna, S., & Verba, M. (1983). *Les bébés entre eux.* Paris: Presses Universitaires de France.

Sutton-Smith, B. (1971). The role of play in cognitive development. In R. E. Herron and B. Sutton-Smith (Eds.), *Child's play.* New York: Wiley.

Tinbergen, N. (1963). On aims and methods of ethology. *Zeitschrift fuer Tierpsychologie, Tierernaehrung und Futtermittelkunde, 20*, 410–432.

Veneziano, E. (1988). Vocal–verbal interaction and the construction of early lexical knowledge. In M. Smith and J. Locke (Eds.), *The emergent lexicon: The child's development of a linguistic vocabulary.* San Diego: Academic Press.

Veneziano, E. (1982). Les échanges conversationnels mère–enfant et les débuts du langage. *Bulletin d'Audiophonologie, 2–3*, 241–262.

Verba, M. (1981). L'organisation des activités prélogiques chez les bébés iraniens. *Enfance, 4–5,* 253–270.

Verba, M., Stambak, M., & Sinclair, H. (1982). Physical knowledge and social interactions. In G. E. Forman (Ed.), *Action and thought.* New York: Academic Press.